Present Like a Pro

Present Like a Pro

The Modern Guide to Getting Your Point Across in Meetings, Speeches, and the Media

Carl Hausman

 PRAEGER ™

An Imprint of ABC-CLIO, LLC

Santa Barbara, California • Denver, Colorado

Library of Congress Cataloging-in-Publication Data

Names: Hausman, Carl, 1953- author.
Title: Present like a pro : the modern guide to getting your point across in
    meetings, speeches, and the media / Carl Hausman.
Description: Santa Barbara, California : Praeger, [2017] | Includes
    bibliographical references and index.
Identifiers: LCCN 2016042048 (print) | LCCN 2016056962 (ebook) |
    ISBN 9781440853289 (hardcopy : alk. paper) | ISBN 9781440853661 (pbk. : alk. paper) |
    ISBN 9781440853296 (eBook)
Subjects: LCSH: Business presentations. | Public speaking. | Business communication. |
    Public relations.
Classification: LCC HF5718.22 .H39 2017 (print) | LCC HF5718.22 (ebook) |
    DDC 658.4/52—dc23
LC record available at https://lccn.loc.gov/2016042048

ISBN: 978-1-4408-5328-9 (hardcover)
ISBN: 978-1-4408-5366-1 (paperback)
EISBN: 978-1-4408-5329-6

21 20 19 18 17   1 2 3 4 5

This book is also available as an eBook.

Praeger
An Imprint of ABC-CLIO, LLC

ABC-CLIO, LLC
130 Cremona Drive, P.O. Box 1911
Santa Barbara, California 93116-1911
www.abc-clio.com

Contents

Expanded Contents

Introduction

Thank you for reading this book, and while it really needs no introduction, without further ado let me YOU'RE ALREADY ZONED OUT, AREN'T YOU?

Of course you are. I began with three droning clichés, which of course led you to believe that you were being served up yet another bland and indifferent word salad, presented timidly and tepidly—in other words, the standard fare served up by most people who are compelled to give a presentation without the proper training.

It doesn't have to be this way. I can teach you how to become an excellent presenter, and I can do it by showing you 10 basic techniques, each broken down into 10 digestible and easily enacted steps.

There is nothing gimmicky or superficial about this approach. All skills involve learning and applying technique, one step at a time. But many people called upon to present have been given no explicit guidance, or—worse, perhaps—have been subjected to instruction from books and seminars that are long on theory about getting your point across but short on clear direction on *exactly how to do it*.

Present Like a Pro does tell you *precisely* how to:

- Plan a presentation (using standard formulas you probably didn't even know existed),
- Galvanize attention with powerful opens and closes,
- Handle tough crowds,
- Develop a powerful speaking voice,
- Deftly employ presentation technology,

- Use humor effectively and without risk, and
- Not only overcome stage fright but also use it to your advantage.

I also provide you with some templates for common presentations and show many examples of how and why presentations motivate, inform, and persuade.

And, as a bonus, *Present Like a Pro* shows you how to be a pioneer in a trend that increasingly dominates the world of business and professional presentation: appearing and presenting on media in interviews, YouTube videos, podcasts, and audiobooks. Moreover, I demonstrate how new digital media can allow you to create something of a small-scale personal media empire, and how to use the synergy of your media to not only bolster public recognition but possibly move you into the realm of professional speaking.

I know how to show you all of this because I've done it, and I know how to teach it because I've done that, too. I've made my living as a lecturer, professor, and writer, with more than ten books about communication skills under my byline. I've appeared on network TV, testified before Congress, worked on-air in television and radio, and narrated several audiobooks.

Before you begin with the first of the 10 techniques, let me address my seeming obsession with the number 10. I've become convinced that humans are hardwired to think and absorb in increments of 10. Maybe it's because of that 10-finger thing—which, after all, did give birth to our entire number system and the digital universe ("digit" means "finger," by the way). I don't view it as a coincidence that there are 10 Commandments, 10 amendments to the Bill of Rights, and tens of millions of top-10 lists everywhere on the Internet, and that the dean of a college gets that title from a Latin word that means "leader of 10," the same root that provides us with the English words "decade" and "deacon." (The Romans were really hung up on units of 10 and based their social and military order on it, so if I'm obsessive, at least I have historical precedent.)

But I think I'll win you over if you take a look at the table of contents. You'll see how each chapter and step provides just enough information to give you a complete picture of what you'll be doing, but not so much that you get lost in the weeds.

Everything is useful, and everything is calculated to help you move forward one step at a time and to reinforce previous learning.

And last but not least, let me take this opportunity to reinforce the fact that you should never use clichés like "last but not least."

How to Use This Book

You are free to access the material in any order you want—after all, it's your book. You paid for it. Thanks, by the way. But I humbly recommend that you read it straight through.

There's an underlying strategy to the order of the techniques and steps: They are arranged in a need-to-know basis, meaning that the most basic and helpful material is presented first, and everything builds in sequence.

I've tried to keep cross-referencing to a minimum because it can be distracting, but it's necessary in cases where relevant information has been or will be presented. References to other chapters will cite both the chapter and step, such as "See Chapter 3, Step 4," but references to numbered steps within the same chapter will include only the step number: "See Step 4."

Throughout the book I provide as many examples as reasonable without breaking up the flow of the narrative. You'll find longer examples of the principles in action in Chapter 11, where I take a mixture of outstanding presentations, some newer, some classic, and point out the techniques used in their planning and execution.

With that in mind, let's begin at the logical first step: How to plan what you're going to say . . .

Chapter 1

Plan It Like You're Patton: Determine Your Battle Plan—Map Out Exactly What You Want to Do and How You Will Do It

I did not intend to inflict upon you Ben Franklin's bromide about how those who fail to plan, plan to fail, but I can't avoid it.

So there.

Having dispensed with that obligation, let me stress that planning a presentation does not have to be an intricate or tedious process. Follow the steps in this chapter, and you can draw up a plan in just a few minutes. Your blueprint can incorporate strategies that have proven effective for centuries—I mean that literally—and can save you stress, tedium, false starts, and embarrassment.

Almost any plan is better than no plan. Plans don't have to be complex.

Your plan can be as simple as "beginning, middle, and end." That was good enough for Aristotle, and he did okay in the presentation department, I've been told. The most famous orator in history, Cicero, advocated a grand total of six parts to a presentation: an introduction, a summary statement of the case you are trying to make, major points in your case, refuting opposing points, crowing about how you have just refuted those points, and a conclusion in which you show how you have made your case.

There are many templates that have proven effective for master presenters, and this chapter will show you how to pick one and adapt it to your needs.

Some of the following ten steps involve structure, and others involve planning for the physical presentation. Employ whichever tactics work for you. Plan as far in advance as feasible, because having a general idea of the structure and content puts your brain on autopilot during the time leading up to the actual presentation. You'll hear or read things that will be perfect for your performance and robotically vacuum them up; moments of inspiration will come to you while standing in line at the bank or sitting in traffic.

Don't get lost in the details, and don't obsess about planning to the point where you come down with a case of perfection paralysis. Just do it, and start now.

To paraphrase Gen. George S. Patton, a good plan executed right now is better than a perfect plan executed next week.

1. DETERMINE YOUR MAIN TAKEAWAY AND WRITE IT IN ONE SENTENCE; IF YOU CAN'T, NO ONE WILL GET YOUR POINT

Here is my main takeaway for this chapter:

This chapter will show you how planning your presentation around some proven steps and strategies can help you re-create the success of others and give your presentation a compelling structure.

You now know the main point, the primary benefit I promise to impart in this chapter. You know what's coming, I know where I'm going, and we are both presumably happy about it.

To continue my militaristic riff on the importance of planning, note that when Dwight Eisenhower (who had once worked as a speechwriter himself and was later schooled in the importance of clear and evocative communication as supreme Allied commander in the Mediterranean and European theaters) assumed the presidency, he demanded that his speechwriters shape his presentations around *one bottom line*—one message the listeners would take home with them. According to James C. Humes, an Eisenhower scholar as well as a master presidential speechwriter, Eisenhower told writers that if they could not put the bottom-line message on the back of a matchbook before they sat down, they were essentially wasting their time.[1]

So save yourself false starts, and draft your takeaway before you begin anything else. Then make sure your entire presentation somehow relates to the takeaway and reinforces it.

Your takeaway can be about 20 words:

- This is a marvelous product, and we will not only make a big profit but also change the industry.
- I am the best candidate for this office because I am beholden to no one and have only your best interests at heart.
- We must fight as hard as we can, because the stakes are so high and the consequences so dire.
- If we set aside our differences, everyone can move forward and accomplish great things.

2. REMEMBER THAT A PRESENTATION IS A JOURNEY: PLAN WHERE YOU WANT TO START, WHERE YOU WANT TO GO, AND WHERE YOU WANT TO END

Every compelling story has movement within its structure. You probably can recognize these common structures from films and mythology:

- Boy meets girl, boy loses girl, boy retrieves girl.
- Mythic hero has a call to adventure, is convinced to step up to the plate by a mentor, begins a quest, overcomes enemies, endures an ordeal, narrowly escapes death, and returns to ordinary life a victor and a wiser person.

And every compelling presentation has a structure too. Here are a couple of examples:

- Introduce your main argument, state your case, outline your main points, prove your case, counter conflicting arguments, and conclude by showing how you have made your case.
- Start with a story illustrating a problem, leave the audience in suspense as to the resolution of the problem, describe possible solutions, refute objections, funnel your audience toward agreeing with your proposed solution, and close with the opening story—how the person you are using for illustration overcame the problem.

None of these structures is complicated or new. The first example above (Introduce your main argument, state your case, outline your main points, etc.) was devised more than two thousand years ago by the Roman orator Cicero and became the basis for Western classical rhetoric—the art of verbal persuasion and motivation.

We'll look at structures in detail later in this chapter and throughout the book, but for now just keep in mind that everything has a structure: pop music, TV sitcoms, symphonies, and speeches. You may not be able to perceive the structure because it seems so natural, but that's the nature of a useful structure—it seems natural and doesn't call attention to itself.

Your favorite song on the radio doesn't sound to you like intro/first verse/chorus/second verse/second chorus/eight bars of variation on the melody/third chorus/closing chorus, does it? But that is a very common underlying structure—so common that people in the music industry will abbreviate it and say, "Here's a song that's a plain old ABABCBB." (If you don't believe me, listen to a few songs on the car radio on the way home; you'll see how many songs fall into this pattern.)

Again, one presentation structure is not inherently better than another, although it might be better suited to a particular application. The important factor is to have some sort of structure designed to carry you through from beginning to middle to end with some sort of perceptible motion and closure.

Note that this advice applies to any sort of communication that you can conceivably classify as a presentation: speech, training session, on-camera response to a media inquiry, podcast, and so forth.

3. INVENTORY THE KNOWLEDGE, NEEDS, AND INTEREST LEVEL OF YOUR AUDIENCE

First figure out where to start in terms of the complexity of the information you'll present. You can't start above the heads of your audience, but you certainly don't want to tell them what they already know. To complicate matters, audiences will often have mixed levels of expertise and experience, so you'll need to acknowledge that: "Some of you certainly know this already, but some won't, so let me briefly review." It's probably best to pitch the content a little above the heads of some while giving occasional catch-up explanations.

Next, consider what the audience needs to get out of it, and gear your approach accordingly. Do they need an understanding of a subject that will allow them to pass a certification test? An understanding of how the *test* works, so that they can apply existing knowledge and pass it? Or do they need to be fired up? Or entertained? Or both?

How much does the audience care about your subject? If the answer is "not a lot," is it worth pursuing? If it's worth it, how can you convince them to care?

Gathering this information isn't that hard. Just talk with the organizers or members of the group. Ask these questions:

- Why will the audience be here? Are they forced to come? Voluntarily coming because they are interested?
- What do they need to know?
- Why do they need to know it? Curiosity? To make more money? Not to be at a disadvantage when competing with others?
- How much do they know now?
- What's the variation in the audience's level of understanding? In other words, will they all be novices? Experts? Half experts and half novices?

4. BE FOCUSED ON THE AUDIENCE'S NEEDS: WHAT'S IN IT FOR THEM?

Your listeners will always be appreciative if you give them something they want. To be fair, what they want might not always be obvious, and the audience members might not be sure of it themselves. You need to clarify the benefit to them, deliver, and make it clear that they will gain something from what you offer.

For example, one of the best performances I ever saw was a presentation on how to give a presentation. The salient point was to capture attention with a good opening and not clutter it up by droning meaningless thank-yous and chitchat at the beginning. The presenter was greeted with polite applause as he took the lectern, but he cut it off and said, "I haven't earned that yet. But I will."

And he went right into his speech—a crackling cascade of useful information, beginning with the lesson to start the speech cold and not to thank people. Save the thanks for later.

The point is that I had a general idea of what I needed to know—more on how to polish a presentation—but not the specifics. The presenter had a fair idea that most of the audience members were relatively experienced communicators who didn't require elementary instruction but needed some quick techniques to up their games. So he provided us with a technique that works well in the hands of a reasonably competent presenter, he did it right off the bat, and by doing so he captured our attention at the beginning so he could effectively lead us through the middle and the end.

Businesses and organizations routinely do what they call "needs assessments" to figure out what their customers want. It becomes a jargon-heavy process, with "needs" sometimes defined as essential things for "well-being" or things that will create a state of "deficiency or deprivation" if denied.[2]

You can assess the needs of your audience by doing surveys or, using a low-tech method that always appealed to me, just talking to people.

Advertising agencies typically convene focus groups to talk to people and learn about the needs of their audience. Let me tell you one story that perfectly illustrates what you're trying to do in a needs assessment. Back in the 1990s, something called the California Milk Processor Advisory Board hired a veteran advertising executive to help stanch the loss of customers for milk. The problem was that choices of beverages were multiplying exponentially with the introduction of new soda flavors and invented beverages such as sports drinks. But there is not a lot you can do with milk. You can flavor it with chocolate or strawberry, but beyond that, it would just get weird. Nobody's going to drink carbonated milk, for example. Milk isn't much of a sports drink, because it doesn't keep forever; it is therefore not really portable.

So, we know that most milk consumption takes place in the home—but what spurs people to buy it? What are their needs? A San Francisco advertising agency set up focus groups (supervised conversations with groups of typical customers) to find out.

The groups didn't produce much that was useful until something happened by accident: It was getting late, and one participant noted that if he didn't leave in time to make it to the store to buy milk, there would be hell to pay the next morning.

And there you have one of the Eureka Moments of needs assessments. What motivates many people to want to buy milk, the conveners of the focus group learned, is *the fear of what happens if they run out*. (I don't know about you, but when my children were little and I didn't have milk, they appeared ready to call a social service agency and report me.)

You know the rest of the story, because you certainly remember the "Got Milk" commercials: entertaining mini-dramas in which a man can't win a telephone quiz contest because when the phone rings, he is chewing on a peanut butter sandwich and has run out of milk with which to wash it down. Another commercial features a snarling business executive who is run over by a bus and winds up in what appears to be a big kitchen in the sky, fully stocked with milk cartons and giant chocolate-chip cookies.

"Heaven," he muses, stuffing himself. And then, naturally, he reaches for the milk carton. But it's empty. And so are all the rest.

The realization is horrifying. "Where am I?" he asks, as flames begin to engulf the "Got Milk" logo.

And there you have the central lesson in needs assessment. Deduce what scares people, what they feel deprived without.

Figure out what causes pain—and offer a solution.

Maybe you'll have to explain to your audience precisely why they should feel deprived, or why they should worry, and that's okay. But without that hook, without that perceived need you are filling, the audience will have no real interest in listening to you.

So, gauge as best you can what your audience needs. Talk with the event organizer or with people who will be at the meeting. What bothers them? What solution are they seeking, and what is the problem they want to solve?

Maybe it is something general and nonspecific: They are tense and upset, and they need a laugh. Or it could be a precise fear: They are worried about meeting sales quotas and need some advice on how to head off failure. Or they are concerned about a new policy, and they *need* assurance that it will be in their best interests. It could be the case that they are worried about loss of productivity in their office, and they *need* the type of product you just happen to sell. Or possibly they are concerned about giving a presentation, in which case you can advise them to buy this book.

5. RUTHLESSLY NARROW YOUR FOCUS AND THE AMOUNT OF MATERIAL

Here are three immutable facts of life. Let's call them Hausman's laws:

Law 1: Everyone worries about having too little material for a presentation and running short.
Law 2: *Nobody* ever has too little material and runs short.

But because people relentlessly continue to believe in Law 1, we inescapably come to …

Law 3: A lot of people giving presentations therefore have way too much they want to cover, they try to cram in and regurgitate too much information, and thus they turn the occasion into a desultory data dump. And they talk too quickly as a result of their panic to wedge everything in.

It's reasonable that you will start with too much material to cram into a presentation. In fact, that's the way it should be. I won't invent any more laws, but if I did, the next one would be something like, "Whether in an article, book, or presentation, you know the content is going to be good when you have too much good information and it becomes difficult to pare it down." So feel free to collect a huge pile of facts and figures for your presentation, but chop down the pile relentlessly until every piece of material sticks to the spine of your main takeaway, until they all fit into your organizational structure and are relevant to your audience's knowledge level and needs.

6. DECIDE ON THE FORMAT THAT WORKS FOR YOU: READING FROM A SCRIPT, BULLET POINTS, CUE CARDS, MEMORIZATION, OR AD-LIBBING

This decision is based partly on the purpose and venue of your presentation and partly on personal preference.

Some decisions regarding format are obvious. You can't show up for a TV interview reading from a script, for example. Some are trickier. If you are giving a presentation about a controversial topic, you are well advised to read from a prepared script so that you won't accidentally say something provocative, and if you are misquoted, you can go back to the text to prove what you said. This isn't timidity—it's good judgment, and you are in good company. Edward R. Murrow followed this route when opening his famous 1954 television takedown of Sen. Joseph McCarthy:

> Good evening. Tonight *See It Now* devotes its entire half hour to a report on Senator Joseph R. McCarthy told mainly in his own words and pictures ... Because a report on Senator McCarthy is by definition controversial, we want to say exactly what we mean to say, and I request your permission to read from the script whatever remarks Murrow and Friendly may make. If the Senator feels that we have done violence to his words or pictures and so desires to speak, to answer himself, an opportunity will be afforded him on this program.[3]

Should you be giving a presentation that will largely be judged on your verbal artistry, you would be well advised to memorize the whole thing. You are probably familiar with TED Talks. TED is an organization that originally held conferences on technology, entertainment, and design (hence the acronym) and now features standout speakers on innovative topics. (There is a TED Talk reprinted in Chapter 11, along with some more information about the organization.) TED Talks are popular on Internet video and on portable audio.

TED organizers generally insist that presenters memorize their speeches and rehearse them many times, word for word. This makes sense because TED talks are more like classical music than improvised jazz. Viewers will be listening for the structure and swell of the presentation, and they expect presenters to hit a bull's-eye every time.

But your presentation actually might be more like a jazz session, with room for improvisation, side trips, and your personal angle on evolving events during the session, such as audience participation. If you're a good ad-libber, consider a series of bullet points to play to your strengths.

The physical form of your notes or script must also be considered. You have many options:

- If you use PowerPoint, Prezi, Keynote, Google Slides, or similar software, viewing your notes from the part of the window only visible to the presenter
- An outline on standard 8 1/2 × 11 paper
- Bullet points
- 3×5 index cards
- Cue cards written on poster board or other large pieces of stiff paper, held up in the audience by a compatriot
- A prompting device, such as a TelePrompTer (TelePrompTer is a trade name referring to a specific brand of prompting device), that electronically scrolls through the script and usually presents it on a panel that is visible to you but not the audience
- A script written in a font large enough for you to comfortably read at arm's length on a lectern. (Note that throughout this book, I'll use "lectern" to indicate the point from where you are speaking, even though it might not always be a lectern. I tend to avoid the words "podium" and "dais" because technically they are structures you stand on.)

As with everything else in life, there are pluses and minuses to each approach. The presenter view in slide software is convenient, in that it comes packaged with the page you are displaying. However, this requires you to be in a position to comfortably view a computer screen—and if there is a problem with the slides, you have a problem with your notes, too. The outline approach tethers you to several pieces of paper but does not do all your thinking for you … you still have to ad-lib. Having said that, it does provide you with a clear structure, making it easy to keep your place and visualize what has been covered and what remains.

Numbers, Roman numerals, and letters can be used in an outline, as can symbols and bullet points. I favor a very simple outlining process, with plain text as the main thought, solid bullets for second-level thoughts, and hollow bullets for third-level ones. This is the default modus operandi of Microsoft Word, saving me the trouble of setting up any special formatting.

I recommend my outline method as a good general-purpose default. It gives me clear prompts and is compact enough so that I can get a sense of the organization of the presentation. For example, here is the opening of a university lecture I give on freedom of the press:

Journalism's existence based on First Amendment
What does it say? - Six clauses:

- *Establishment*
- *Practice*

- *Speech*
- *Press*
- *Assembly*
- *Petition*

However ...

- *Does it mean what it says? How can it?*
- *Why the exceptions? How did it get to where it is today?*

Start with the Backstory ...

- *Begins with tussle between freedom and oppression, and also technology and oppression ...*
  - *People not born with rights*
  - *Magna Carta 1215*
  - *Petition of Right, 1628, cited Magna Carta as precedent*

Occasionally I have used bullet points on 3 × 5 index cards. Index cards fit easily into a pocket and thus are inconspicuous, and the points can easily be mixed and matched and shuffled around to customize the presentation. Unfortunately, it's easy for me to inadvertently shuffle the cards—generally by dropping them—so I avoid this method.

Cue cards written on large pieces of cardboard are visible to an audience and can appear awkward and even comical, but they remain a good low-tech method for referring to notes when giving a presentation involving video cameras (in other words, you are concerned about what the camera sees, not what the audience, if any, sees). The trick is to be able to read from them while not perceptibly diverting your eyes from the lens. To enable this, keep the cameras and the cards as far from you, the speaker, as practicable. The angle of the eyes is much less visible from a distance as compared to a close-up. Another trick to maintaining the appearance of eye contact with a camera is to mount (or have a compatriot hold) the cards above or below the lens. Upward movement of the eyes is less perceptible than a sideways glance.

Prompting devices cure the problem of eye contact by projecting the script onto a surface that is reflective to the reader but invisible to the audience. They are not readily available, although computer technology using tablets and smartphones hooked up to a small mirror is making prompters more accessible to the general public. The devices also take some practice to use. As a general rule, I steer clear of them unless there is no reasonable alternative. There are too many weak links in the prompting chain, including errors on the part of the operator and technical glitches involving projection of the script and the speed at which it moves.

Typing out the script and reading it provides the presenter with a crutch but at a price: For most people, it is difficult to read a script smoothly and naturally. Having said that, though, there are occasions when you will want the wording to be exact, and printing out a copy in a large enough font to comfortably read is simple. This is a major advantage of the computer; when I first began inflicting myself on audiences, the only option for a speaker who needed large type was a special "Orator" font on a ball that fit into an IBM Selectric typewriter. It's obvious to note that such is not the case today, but less obvious is the fact that the myriad fonts available on a word-processing program have *widely* varying levels of readability. Experiment. Find the size and font that's most effective for you, should you go the route of reading off a script or from bullet points on a printed page. Resist the temptation to use a huge font visible from an orbiting satellite, because you will have to flip pages too often, and you may lose the sense of continuity provided by being able to scan many words on a page. Personally, I like 18-point Times Roman. Times Roman is a serif font, meaning that the letters have little feet. I find that this aids readability, and as I have reasonably good distance vision, I don't need the text to be much bigger, and I like the idea that I can see a fairly large amount of text and notes. Your mileage may vary, so do a lot of experimentation.

7. DECIDE WHETHER TO USE MEDIA, WHAT KIND, AND WHY YOU WANT TO USE IT

Slides and video are terrific. Sometimes. And sometimes they are just awful—even laughable. Google comedian "Don McMillan" and "Death by PowerPoint," and you'll see what I mean.

He cuts pretty close to reality in the opening of his routine when he shows his first PowerPoint slide and reads it word for word. The slide looks like this:

Most Common PowerPoint Mistakes

(1) People tend to put every word they are going to say on their PowerPoint slides. Although this eliminates the need to memorize your talk, ultimately this makes your slides crowded, wordy, and boring. You will lose your audience's attention before you even reach the bottom of your ...[4]

Don't be that guy. Use media sparingly and only when it adds something unique or serves some purpose better than simply talking. We'll look at presentation media in more detail in later chapters, but at this point, here is what you need to know.

Use slides ...

- For titles
- For main points, especially definition of technical terms
- For highlighting a theme or a question that will recur throughout the presentation
- For visuals, when those visuals convey the image better than you can by words alone

Do not use slides ...

- To read from
- As a crutch
- As incessant decoration
- As the primary conveyor of information (If it's essential that people know something that is presented in a written format, give them a handout or a Web link.)
- To echo what you are saying

Use video ...

- When you have video of something to which you are referring (For example, in Technique #6 above, I referred to Edward R. Murrow. Had I been giving a presentation, it certainly would have been a good spot to insert a video clip.)
- When video can provide a brief punctuation (Had I been giving a presentation on the misuse of PowerPoint, I could have effectively used a clip from Don McMillan.)

Do not use video ...

- As a halfway measure between a video presentation and a live presentation (If you want to show a video, fine—show it. If you want to give a presentation with a little bit of video serving as a condiment, that's also fine. But half talk, half video leaves the audience confused.)
- When there is any question as to its relevance

8. REHEARSE LIKE A PROFESSIONAL: MAKE YOURSELF BETTER, AND DON'T PRACTICE YOUR MISTAKES

Rehearsal helps—a lot, much more than you would expect. For one thing, you don't want to present a rough draft to an audience, and you don't want to have a lapse in concentration derail you during an ill-prepared presentation.

Some people reject the idea of rehearsing by insisting that by rehearsing, they will wind up with a rote, canned presentation, and they would rather wing it and give the audience a unique experience. Now, there is something to that argument, but within very limited strictures. I have to admit that some of the greatest performers in history shunned rehearsal. A noted example is Jackie Gleason, who terrified cast members by his last-minute brinksmanship. But his brilliance emanated from walking that same tightrope—the risk gave it an edge.

But remember that Gleason had "rehearsed" his "unrehearsed" performance thousands of times before. He spent more time on stage than most people spend in the office, so he was not exactly inventing each performance anew. Aside from that, he was a genius.

So until you are firmly established as a genius, careful rehearsal is advised. Rehearse your ad-libs, too. (Don't be naïve: *Of course* experienced performers rehearse clever off-the-cuff remarks. That's how they sound witty and off-the-cuff. See Chapter 9, Step 5 for more.)

Some people become discouraged with the results of rehearsal because they do it all wrong. They rush through, delivering their lines in a whisper directed at their chest, ignore the coordination of technology they will be using and what they will say, and get no feedback from an observer. Remember: Without feedback you don't get corrected, and without correction *you practice your mistakes* and become better at *doing it wrong*.

With those points in mind, here are guidelines for rehearsing a presentation so that you'll actually get better, not worse:

- **Video yourself.** In the era of the smartphone and the video camera on almost every laptop sold, there is no reason not to take advantage of this option. Yes, it can be painful to watch, but there is simply no better way to fix weak points. From personal experience I can tell you that even the most masterful broadcast announcers weren't born with their talent. Speaking and reading with accuracy and eloquence *is an acquired skill*; you acquire that skill by practicing, evaluating the results, and making changes and adjustments, just like hitting balls at a driving range, seeing how far they go, and adjusting your stance.
- **Get feedback.** Continuing the golf analogy, anyone who has taken a golf lesson knows the value of feedback. Sometimes you literally can't tell if your own arm is straight, or if you are rocking too much. You may have the same blind spot for speaking too quickly or glossing over the main points. An informed observer can help. If possible, get someone to watch your presentation and provide feedback. (You have nothing to lose: If the person is a jerk, at least you'll have practice handling a heckler.)
- **Rehearse in sections.** In one of my many failed careers, I was an orchestral musician. I attended a master class with a renowned clarinetist who would listen to the student play and then offer advice and play the selection himself.

Some of the music was very challenging, even beyond the capacity of a first-chair musician to sight-read. So he learned it on the spot, in front of a large group of students, and here's how he did it: Instead of charging through the passage, which was about a minute long, he slowly played the first phrase, then speeded it up when he played it once more. He repeated the process with the second phrase (maybe ten seconds of music), and so on. Then he grafted the parts together, playing the first part and the second part, then the first part and the second part and the third part, then the whole thing. The point is that he polished the sections first, slowly and carefully. Then he put them together, building up speed and expression. *That's* what you want to do when you rehearse a speech. Don't try to run through the whole thing, at least not at first. Do it slowly, at least at first, getting the details right so you don't practice your mistakes.

- **Practice more than the words**. Rehearse movements, pauses, inflections, and integration of the technology.

9. WRITE YOUR DRAFT FOR THE EAR, NOT FOR THE EYE

Words that work well on paper do not necessarily translate gracefully to being spoken aloud. If you are writing out your remarks word for word for a formal speech or for a piece you are recording on audio or video, you need to craft words that can comfortably be spoken and listened to.

This isn't complex if you follow these rules:

- **Keep sentences short**. An occasional long sentence is all right (and in fact tends to break up monotonous patterns), but err on the short side.
- **Write in a conversational tone**. Make sure that whatever you write sounds like a normal speech pattern and not an academic journal or a newspaper editorial. The easiest way to assess whether you pass this test is to read things aloud as you write them. If a sentence sounds stilted, start over.
- **Be clear**. Don't write, "As we can see from the latter example," because the listener has no way to replay what you have said to discern the former from the latter.
- **Watch pronouns**. A listener can't go back and figure out who the "he" refers to if you have just mentioned several men. When in doubt, repeat a name rather than use a pronoun.
- **Use contractions**. Forget the admonitions from your seventh-grade English teacher. Contractions are natural in spoken communication. Having said that, be careful of easily misheard words such as "can" and "can't," which sound an awful lot alike when spoken. If it's possible that a listener will be confused, rephrase.
- **Put attribution first**. For example, "Our researchers say this will be the best quarter in the past decade" is easier to say and listen to than "This will be the best quarter in the past decade, our researchers say."

- **Make very short sentences carry the weight**. This is a potent technique and is dirt simple: When you want to make an impact and get across a key point, make it a very short sentence. Compare this uninspired wording . . .

I disagree with our critics who say we won't be able to adapt to the changing technologies because our business is rooted in face-to-face sales. In fact, I would endeavor to say that we may surpass their expectations and turn in a performance better than anything we have done before. By integrating the newest database and contact management technology into our . . .

with this:

Some of our critics say we won't be able to adapt to the changing technologies because our business is rooted in face-to-face sales.
    They are wrong.
    We will succeed beyond anyone's expectations except mine.
    By integrating the newest database and contact management technology into our . . .

10. GEAR EVERYTHING TO YOUR DESIRED OUTCOME—AND REMEMBER THAT J. P. MORGAN HIT IT ON THE HEAD WHEN HE SAID A PERSON HAS TWO REASONS FOR DOING SOMETHING: ONE THAT SOUNDS GOOD, AND THE REAL REASON

Remember, you need everything in your presentation to serve your purpose. If you are giving a campaign speech, for example, you want all of the presentation's elements to impel people to vote for you. If you are making a presentation to a potential customer, you want to sell your product.

At the same time, remember that there are usually many desires and motivations at play in anyone's decision-making process. This really isn't a mysterious progression, and you can probably unravel many of the strings you can pull to subtly influence your audience. Voters, for example, might be looking for a candidate who not only shares their fundamental views (the *ostensible* reason) but also personifies the deep anger they have at a system that many feel has not been working (the *real* reason). A client naturally wants to choose a product that is of high quality (the *ostensible* reason) but also wants to deal with a salesperson who seems reliable, approachable, and likely to untangle the inevitable problems that come with the supply chain (the *real* reason).

Think past the immediate task. Start with your desired result, and then keeping that in mind, reverse-engineer the process of planning your presentation.

Chapter 2

Present It Like It's a Play: Harness the Structural Power of Mini-Acts, Scenes, and Climaxes

Impactful presentations and dramas have a structure that might not be apparent at first glance. But if you look at the studs underneath the structures, you'll find some standard blueprints that you can adapt for your own presentations. You can appropriate the same structural techniques that playwrights use: acts, stories, characters, suspense, impactful silence, memorable phrases, and swelling climaxes.

1. VISUALIZE IT AS THREE ACTS: A GRAND THEME SUPPORTED BY WHAT ARISTOTLE CALLED "THE RULE OF THREE"

Plays have traditionally been structured into three acts, and you can make a case that the most engaging presentations in all media follow this durable structure as well.

In fact, the late Stephen J. Cannell, one of the most prolific scriptwriters in history, argued that "every great movie, book, or play that has withstood the test of time has a solid three-act structure."[1]

Cannell sketched out his interpretation of the three-act structure this way:

Act One: The central character meets the other characters, and we learn the central problem of the story. Act One sets up the viewers or readers, getting

them to like or dislike various characters and to care about their relationships and about solving the main problem.

Act Two: Here we see the problem loom larger, and the hero sets out to solve
the problem and defeat his or her adversaries. But at the end of Act Two,
things go very wrong for our hero, and it looks hopeless . . .

Act Three: The problem is solved. Often, a lesson is learned.

Now, I want to take a side trip here, to a related but not identical subject: "The Rule of Three." Aristotle, the father of persuasive speaking, wrote
about this in his book *Rhetoric*. It's a pretty simple rule: People tend to
remember and react to things when they are presented in groups of three.

I came, I saw, I conquered
Liberty, equality, fraternity
Life, liberty, and the pursuit of happiness
Government of the people, by the people, and for the people

The three-act structure and "The Rule of Three" are not exactly the same
concept, but they're close. I believe that people are hardwired to pay attention to a three-part phrase; more generally, they are drawn to a very simple
structure: (1) beginning, (2) middle, and (3) end.

"Beginning, middle, and end" is useful but a little too general for planning purposes, so instead think back to Cannell and about the *content* of
those three parts:

Beginning: Act One, meeting the characters and understanding the problem
Middle: Act Two, complications and struggle
End: Act Three, problem solved and lesson learned

Get it? On a macro level, you cannot go wrong with a three-part structure (at least in terms of elements related to the structure). And on a micro
level, you cannot go wrong with presenting some of your main ideas within
the presentation in sets of three.

That is so important that I feel compelled to repeat it, using both bold-
face and italics, the writer's telltale indicators of fanaticism:

***On a macro level, you cannot go wrong with a three-part structure. And on
a micro level, you cannot go wrong with presenting some of your main ideas
with the presentation in set of three.***

You can fit *any presentation* into the three-by-three structure, and we
will provide illustrations throughout. The above point is very important,

and alone it is worth the price of this book. However, as my contract calls for a full twelve chapters, I will continue.

2. TELL STORIES, DON'T DUMP DATA

Don Hewitt, the originator of the television news magazine *60 Minutes,* had a simple formula for viewer engagement: He told his reporters to "tell me a story." Facts about the record rainfall may intrigue meteorologists, he might have said, but the travails of a couple who have just seen their home swept away by a wall of water is what rivets the viewer and, more importantly, gets the main point across.

The power of stories is an integral part of human history. Remember that in preliterate times, knowledge was codified into stories and retold aloud. The story became the vehicle for memorization and understanding.

I contend that humans are hardwired to react to stories and learn from them. I made up that claim a couple of years ago because it sounded good when I was lecturing freshmen, but I recently learned that it is literally true. A team of neuroscientists at Princeton used an MRI machine to snoop inside the brains of volunteers who listened, as part of a group, to a storyteller. They found that the subjects' brains not only responded energetically to a skilled storyteller's narrative but also actually "coupled" and responded in unison; the story was almost literally "transferred" to the collective brain of the audience. Also, the brain patterns of the listeners *replicated the brain patterns of the storyteller*—something that did not happen when a speaker was simply relaying facts.[2]

I'll bet that what I just told you got your attention. It was supposed to; it was a *story.* Get it? Instead of relaying a series of facts, I began with my contention that the brain is hardwired for stories, admitted how I used to just assume that, and told how I became convinced based on a story involving Princeton scientists and an MRI.

Moral of the (here comes that word again) *story:* Don't ignore facts and figures, but whenever reasonably possible, tell stories that capture the attention of the listener and illustrate your case.

3. MAKE YOUR AUDIENCE THE MAIN CHARACTERS

What the Princeton experiment really demonstrates is that stories involve the listener in the activity. Involvement is a primary goal for anyone giving a presentation. You want the audience to become part of the presentation.

How do you encourage participation? Depending on your desired outcome, you might, for example, ask your audience questions during the presentation, and when an answer is proffered, ask another audience member what he or she thinks about it. (Don't overdo this, because you run the risk of letting the audience hijack the talk.)

Inc. magazine's Allison Goldberg and Jen Jamila urge speakers to get creative with audience engagement. "For instance," they write, "rather than show everyone that 20% of your demographic thinks one way through a boring slide, try having 20% of them move to one side of the room. Or, have the chairs already set up at 20/80 when people arrive, and at some point ask if they know why they're seated that way. (You could also gift prizes hidden under seats to 20% of the audience, Oprah-style, but we realize this might only be exciting when the loot is a budget-breaking Lexus or cruise vacation.)"[3]

4. CREATE SUSPENSE: THE TECHNIQUE OF TENSION AND RELEASE

A piece of music that is written with the intent of being pleasing throughout will please no one. Composers know that audiences crave a little bit of dissonance (groups of notes that don't sound right together and grate on the ear), repetitive and slightly annoying buildups, continually rising pitches, and other devices that create uncertainty but are *resolved* by the music returning to a pleasant "home" key.

All presentations benefit from a little suspense that is resolved seconds or minutes later. An audience that is never unsettled in the beginning and middle will never be fully settled at the end.

Creating tension and release is not particularly difficult. Does your presentation involve, say, a prop or a product? Keep it in a cardboard box next to you on stage. Talk for several minutes, ignoring the box, waiting for the tension to build, and then release it by retrieving the object. If someone in the audience can't stand it and demands to know what's in the box, you have scored a double victory because you have also recruited some audience involvement.

An unresolved joke is an excellent tension-and-release device. An experienced speaker I recently saw livened up what promised to be a mundane sports banquet by opening with a story of his unhappy career in sports, beginning with a nasty high school coach who snarled at him, warning that he would never be a real ball player unless he could do four things: run, hit, and throw.

The speaker continued on for a minute or two while the audience eventually got the joke, and someone asked what the fourth thing was.

"I'll give you a hint," the speaker said. "It wasn't doing math."

But the speaker hinted that he did learn the fourth requirement and would announce it at the end of his remarks.

That's a pretty much no-lose technique. It's a low-risk type of humor (we'll talk more about humor in Chapter 9), it invokes audience involvement, and it creates two episodes of tension and release.

In sum, don't be reluctant to *plan* to unsettle the audience a little, and hold out the resolution to a question that has been posed or a puzzle that has presented itself, and *you are really getting annoyed with me for not telling you the fourth secret to succeeding in baseball and in life, aren't you*?

It's *the desire to hustle*—"just what you've all shown in (buying this book, winning the scholar athlete award, fill in the blank)."

5. HIT ALL THREE OF THE CLASSIC DRIVERS OF OPINION: *LOGOS, PATHOS, ETHOS*

Aristotle identified three "rhetorical appeals" called *ethos*, *pathos*, and *logos*. He asserted that listeners are persuaded by authority and qualification (*ethos*), appeals to emotion (*pathos*), and demonstrations of logic (*logos*).

He put it this way: "Of the [modes of persuasion] provided through speech there are three species: for some are in the character of the speaker, and some are in disposing the listener in some way, and some in the argument itself, by showing or seeming to show something."[4]

Allow me to simplify: If you want your presentation to unfold dramatically and move the audience to your point of view, you must work in material that establishes your credibility, touches the audience in some way, and ends with a conclusion that at least has the appearance of being logically derived.

It's not that hard; just make sure you check the *ethos*, *pathos*, and *logos* boxes at some point. You don't have to go overboard. For example, you can establish your *ethos* by briefly pointing out how long you've been involved with a particular cause or business, or noting how you have been personally affected by the issue at hand. *Pathos* (a Greek word meaning "suffering" or "experience") is evoked by stories (see Step 2 above), and you can briefly illustrate your case with an anecdote. *Logos* often comes in the closing argument, where you indicate that everything you've said adds up to your conclusion.

You can manage to check all three boxes even in a one-minute presentation at a city council meeting:

> *I've operated a small business in the city's central business district for more than 20 years* (ethos) *and have seen firsthand the corrosive effects of the property taxes in that area. The businesses immediately to the right and the left of me have closed.*

Both were family-run businesses, and the owner of one of them now tells me he won't be able to pay for his son's college (pathos). But this affects more than just the business owners: People just won't come into the center city anymore if there is nothing there for them! I realize that tax abatements for this district will result in a small, short-term loss of tax revenue, but not doing something about the problem will eventually dry up all *tax revenues from the area. Kicking the can down the road just doesn't make economic sense (logos).*

6. EXPLOIT THE POWER OF SILENCE

Silence is one of the most powerful yet most underutilized tools available to the presenter. Script your silences for maximum impact. For example, in the one-minute masterpiece above, you could add considerable impact this way:

I realize that tax abatements for this district will result in a small, short-term loss of tax revenue, but not doing something about the problem [pause for three seconds, scanning the room . . . then lean forward] will eventually dry up all *tax revenues from the area.*

Silence makes people uncomfortable. Admit it. Think about all the stupid things you've said to fill awkward silences during blind dates, for example. ("Uh . . . look what I stepped in on the way over . . .") But momentary discomfort is *good* for a presenter because it galvanizes attention, and you can use the tension-and-release technique described above to resolve the point dramatically.

One of the greatest speakers of modern times, Edward R. Murrow, made silence his trademark. His landmark radio reports from wartime Europe began as follows:

This [pause] is London.

The pause was added at the urging of his college public-speaking teacher, who recognized the dramatic effect that could be injected by scripting silence.

Should you need to evoke a response from the group or person to whom you are presenting, silence can be a powerful persuader. The entrepreneur Daniel Tenner notes that silence

. . . can be a very useful tool for sales, for example: when you're trying to close a sale, at one point you need to state your pitch, with the price, and then just shut up. If you keep talking, you will only distract the customer from evaluating the pitch and coming to a decision.

In person-to-person conversations, few people can tolerate a prolonged silence, particularly when it follows a certain kind of statement. "I don't know what I can do to solve X," *followed by uncomfortable silence,* will often pull suggestions for solving X out of someone who would not have volunteered them if simply confronted by a direct question.[5]

7. PLAN THREE MEMORABLE PHRASES AND BUILD YOUR PRESENTATION AROUND THEM

Remember this about remembering: Audiences don't remember much. They will generally have better recall of material at the beginning and the end, and will take away memories of the highlights of the presentation. The rest often becomes a blur, so you need to help them remember your highlights by *planning the highlights in advance.*

What makes a memorable highlight? Usually it's a clever turn of phrase, something witty that reinforces your main points. For example, I occasionally give presentations on abuse of statistics. If you think this has the potential to be dull, you are correct. But I can usually garner some attention by saying a variation of this sometime near the opening of my remarks:

Statistics are like bikinis. What they reveal is enticing, but what they conceal is vital.

You'd be surprised how often that gets quoted after I make a speech or television appearance. It's not Shakespeare, I grant you, but it works.

If you are giving a presentation of more than a few minutes, try for three memorable phrases. The two others I usually use in a speech about statistics are as follows:

Half-truths have become the coin of the realm in the persuasion business, and like a Gresham's Law of Information, bad information drives out good.

Advertisers trade in veiled variables and confusing counterfeits.

The latter phrase takes advantage of the memorability of alliteration (repeating beginning letters).

Having trouble coming up with your own memorable phrases? Use a quote. Do a Web search to unearth pithy quotes about your subject. Generally, you want to credit the source of your quote (although in the interest of full disclosure, I have a feeling I heard the bikini quote elsewhere and adopted it but have not bothered to check), and you are well advised to verify the quote from a couple different sources.

I say that because some quotes are erroneously attributed, either accidentally or on purpose. A wonderful quote I've used in the statistics speech is often attributed to Mark Twain:

It ain't what you don't know that gets you into trouble. It's what you know for sure that just ain't so.

But is sometimes attributed to Will Rogers. I don't know the answer, but some folks who apparently have a lot of time on their hands have combed through the entire history of the spoken and written word and determined that the quote actually comes from no one in particular.[6]

Be very careful of any political quote—especially something your crazy uncle posted on Facebook—because those are sometimes created of whole cloth and are falsely attributed.

8. ALTERNATE BETWEEN PROBLEM AND SOLUTION

We love solutions to problems. Life is a continual quest for solutions to problems. As a presenter, you can appeal to this tendency by embarking on a quest to identify problems for which you can offer the solutions.

For example, to continue the discussion of my stock presentation on statistics (which I use for illustration because understanding statistics is one of the most unappealing subjects imaginable), I don't promise the audience I am going to make them more agile in interpreting statistics. Nobody cares about that.

But *everyone* cares about fixing a problem. One problem, as I tell the audience, is that they are continually hoodwinked by misleading statistics in advertising for financial services, airline flights, hotel rooms, and the like. And what I have to offer is a *solution*: how to keep from getting ripped off.

I stress this as part of the "Present It Like It's a Play" chapter because every drama is about overcoming a problem. If there's not a problem, it's not a drama; and if it's not a drama, no one will stay awake for the second act. So take advantage of the problem/solution structure: one big problem and one big solution, multiple problems and multiple solutions offered in alternating sequence, or—and this is very effective—multiple problems fixed by one big solution.

9. USE THE PLAYWRIGHT'S AND COMPOSER'S TRICK OF "FALSE ENDINGS" TO BUILD AUDIENCE ANTICIPATION AS YOU APPROACH THE CONCLUSION

The key to a dramatic presentation is buildup to a climax, but no one has the patience to sit still through a work of any fairly substantial length that is all one big buildup. You keep audience attention by building in mini-climaxes along the way. You have a great deal of flexibility in doing this. For example, you might use a strategy mentioned above and offer a series of problems and a series of solutions, building up to one grand unifying theory to solve all problems in the universe, in which case I would appreciate you contacting me through my Web site and telling me what it is.

A dangling joke (where you don't reveal the entire punch line right away, as discussed in Step 4 above) works well.

As you move toward the conclusion, throw in a couple false endings. You are familiar with false endings from music and movies. In music, a false ending is where the chords and melody build toward an apparent conclusion, only to retreat back to a reiteration of the main melodic theme. This injects some additional suspense and tension into the music. And we are all familiar with the film device where the dull-witted teenagers escape peril, wipe their brows, congratulate each other, and then bump into another guy with a chainsaw.

You don't have to craft an intricate plot line to build in false endings and revive and keep audience attention during the last quarter of a presentation. Just say "in conclusion" when you have five minutes left. Say it again when you have two minutes left. (Watch political speeches; this is done all the time. I once counted nine "in conclusions" at a presidential nominating convention speech.)

If you want an alternative to "in conclusion," try these:

- *If you take nothing else away from this talk . . .*
- *My ultimate point . . .*
- *The most important thing I can leave you with . . .*

10. BRING THE CURTAIN UP ON TIME (BUT BE PREPARED TO FUDGE WITH THE "NETWORKING" GIMMICK IF THERE ARE UNAVOIDABLE DELAYS)

And to conclude with the play analogy, let me point out that one of the more difficult aspects of a play, concert, or any public performance is getting it started. If a sizable share of the audience is filing in while the presentation is beginning, the atmosphere becomes chaotic, and you may be compelled to repeat your opening remarks. However, if you wait too long to start, you risk alienating the people who got there on time—and you will thus begin with a semi-hostile audience.

In the longer term, constantly starting late in reaction to late-arriving audience members habituates the rest of the audience to showing up late—something to think about if you are giving a regular series of trainings or classes. You can eventually train (most of) an audience to arrive on time.

Broadway shows usually start within a few minutes of the scheduled curtain time, and so the audience remembers. (The reason for Broadway's famed punctuality is probably economic. With union-staffed theaters, the crew goes into expensive overtime beyond a standard period, usually three hours.[7])

Sometimes half the audience will arrive late through no fault of their own. Perhaps there has been a delay with the previous session. What do you do?

- First, note how cleverly I used a problem/solution framework to focus your attention, so please send me e-mail congratulating me.
- When you are actually beginning, have someone introduce you if at all possible, even if you are supposed to be starting the event. That builds in a buffer and allows you to stall without you having to do the stalling. Your introducer can kill time with remarks about the schedule, upcoming events, or other housekeeping details.
- If there is a good reason why the audience is late, you can simply state that and apologize for the delay. Audiences are more understanding of waiting times if they are not kept in the dark as to the reason.
- If it is appropriate for your audience, ask them to do a little networking while they are waiting. You can even facilitate this by moving from table to table, offering introductions, and encouraging conversation.

Chapter 3

Magnify Your Message with Credibility, Approachability, and Listenability

We've covered the basics of planning, constructing, and scripting the presentation (though there is more advanced information, including the fine points of openings and closings, to come in later chapters).

This chapter will focus on the fundamentals of delivering a presentation before a live audience. Using presentation technology and appearing on media will be covered in later chapters.

Here are the steps to follow to maximize your delivery.

1. BEGIN WITH THE THREE RULES OF A COHERENT AND ENGAGING TALK: SLOW DOWN, SLOW DOWN, AND SLOW DOWN SOME MORE

Speed kills credibility and audience engagement. *Slow down!*

Remember that in addition to causing incomprehensibility, "fast-talking" is associated with dishonesty, so rattling through your presentation calls your sincerity into question.

Too rapid a pace sometimes stems from fear that you'll lose an audience if you don't regurgitate information quickly enough. Realistically, that won't happen, and you stand a better chance of losing them if they can't follow you. In other cases, machine-gun deliveries are symptomatic of a nervous meltdown—an indicator that the speaker is losing control. It can convey the image that you believe that what you have to say is unimportant and you want to get it over with.

There is a bona fide speech disorder called "cluttering," in which groups of words are mashed together. If you suspect that is the case, you might approach a speech-language pathologist (a specialist in voice and speech with a master's degree and a national certification).

But for most people, the cure for excessive speed is simply a matter of reminding yourself—and forcing yourself—to slow down.

If you want a trick or device to slow you down, try these:

- **Write a reminder directly into your script or notes.** A visual reminder popping up from time to time is helpful. Even the best of us need a cue; President Eisenhower was notorious for rambling on, so his handlers had a special plate attached to his lectern that would light up and demand, "GET OFF NOW." In comparison, writing "SLOW DOWN' on page 3 of your script is not such an imposition.
- **Breathe more deeply and more often**. Breath control is essential to magnifying voice power (among the topics covered in Chapter 7), but taking regular, deep breaths calms you and effortlessly slows your pace, because you can't talk and breathe at the same time.
- **Insert pauses**, as recommended in Chapter 2, Step 6. Pauses offer the dual benefit of adding drama and slowing down speech.
- **Time yourself reading from a script, and observe your words-per-minute rate so you will have a consistent measure to shoot for**. I like to keep my rate for audiobooks, online narration, and most public speaking at about 150 words per minute. Your mileage may vary depending on the circumstances, but 150 is a good starting point. Hitting it is easier than it sounds: When you rehearse, simply set your smartphone timer for a minute, count 150 words into your presentation, mark that spot, and read. If you finish before hitting the marker, slow down. If you drag on much longer than the marker, chug a couple cups of coffee and rev up the speed. Keep practicing to hit the target, and after a few sessions, that rhythm will be imprinted in your neurons and you will be able to summon it naturally.

2. ADOPT THE POWER POSE THAT RESEARCH SHOWS TO BE MOST EFFECTIVE

You are probably familiar with the work of Amy Cuddy, who became famous for her TED Talk on body language. If you haven't seen it, just google her name and the phrase "power poses." It's well worth the 20-minute time investment.

In essence, Cuddy maintains that her research demonstrated that erect poses with arms away from the body communicate a sense of power, so much so that subjects who practiced these poses actually *felt* more powerful. One of Cuddy's favorites was the hands-on-hips "Wonder Woman" pose (which, if I understand her research correctly, is of more use for psyching yourself up than as an actual presentation posture).

In actuality, I believe that for the purposes of presentation, any posture that involves keeping the head up, the shoulders squared, the feet firmly planted, and the back straight will not only communicate an aura of power but also help you maintain energy and project your voice.

It's really about *conveying that you are confident and in control*. Any posture that sends that message will serve its purpose, and you don't have to stand like the Statue of Liberty to achieve it. You may remember William F. Buckley, one of the great speakers of all time; he would slouch when standing, and sometimes when hosting his television show, he would recline sideways in his chair to the point where he appeared ready to slide off. But he was deliberate in these postures, not fidgeting or trying to find a place to put his hands or hunching up his shoulders.

So concentrate on posture that communicates *ease and command*. Generally, head up, shoulders back, and back straight is as good as anything else. Remember not to make continual fidgety movements, as that conveys a lack of confidence and is visually distracting. Above all, do not lean into the microphone in what I call the "nibbling bird" posture. Adjust the stand so you can stand erect and talk comfortably. With most microphones, you do not have to have your mouth extremely close to have it work properly. And if proximity to the microphone is essential, you are better off holding the microphone in your hand if you can.

3. MOVE WITH A PURPOSE: USE POWERFUL GESTURES AND WORK THE ROOM GRACEFULLY

Appropriate and expressive gestures enhance engagement, but repetitive gestures are distracting, fidgety gestures indicate a lack of self-confidence, and exaggerated gestures make the speaker appear out of control.

Here are five guidelines for using gestures to your advantage:

- **Remember to keep scale appropriate**. If you are giving a speech in a hall with two balconies, grand gestures are okay. But in a small room or—worse—on television, expansive movement appears manic. Have a colleague stand where you will be stationed, while you scope out the venue. You'll get an idea how much movement is needed. If you're performing on video, find out what the standard shots will be and adjust your movements accordingly. In general, less—much less—is more when it comes to televised gestures.

- **Be careful of mannerisms.** I used to have a professor who would punctuate each and every sentence with a palsied karate chop. We would imitate him in class, in the hall, and at frat parties. Don't be that guy. A distinctive gesture is fine—in fact, you might want to develop one as a trademark—but when it is overused, the gesture becomes distracting at best and fodder for ridicule at worst.

- **Along the same lines, make sure gestures have purposes.** If you want to stab a finger at the audience to make an appropriate point ("and you have been cheated time and time again by this insane policy . . .") that's fine. But if the gesture habitually persists through a joke or a tribute to a fallen friend, you are sending mixed and confusing signals. This might actually be a bigger problem than you suspect, because sometimes people subconsciously read things into inappropriate gestures, and they may not even be aware of their reaction; all they know is that something is wrong. I once knew someone who kept his fists clenched during even the lightest parts of his presentations. I don't know if the mismatched gesture was symptomatic of anything, and it took me a while to figure out what the dissonance in his appearance was, but I believe his habit made people uneasy even if they could not put their fingers on what was bothering them.

- **Maintain an arsenal of functional and appropriate gestures.** Two that work well are (1) hands in front of body and spread, palms out, when addressing the audience and (2) palms turned in when talking about yourself. I like listing points from time to time and using fingers to count them out. (Just don't use this technique for 11 or more points.) Some speaking coaches advise against using clenched fists or pointed fingers, but if those gestures are used with sincerity and not in a hostile way, they can be very effective. An arm outreached to the audience in a gesture that looks like you are inviting someone to dance is an excellent device to implore listeners to join you in a belief or idea.

- **Full-body gestures, when appropriate for the venue, work well.** For example, if you want to make a final appeal to the audience, get out from behind the lectern, move to the edge of the stage, and use the come-and-dance gesture with one arm while holding the microphone in the other hand. If you are wearing a microphone and are not tethered to one location, moving around the stage or platform is an excellent option, as long as you don't pace mechanically. If you are comfortable doing so, opt for a location that does not plant you behind a lectern; it's just one more barrier between you and the audience. If you have notes but no formal lectern, you can put them on a music stand and refer to them occasionally. I believe that one of the most physically inviting setups for a speaker is a simple stool, a music stand, and a handheld mic. It communicates to the audience that you are not afraid of them and not desirous of a barrier, and it allows you the freedom to sit and then stand when you want to punctuate an idea.

4. MAINTAIN EYE CONTACT THROUGH PLANNED FOCUS POINTS

If an audience is large, obviously you cannot maintain eye contact with every member. However, you can give *the impression* of engaging in individual eye contact with these mechanisms:

- **Pick several locations where you will routinely focus on an audience member**—direct front, left rear, right front, right rear center, etc. The point is that you don't want to forget about a section of the audience, something that's easy to do in the heat of battle. Practice your sectors in advance until it becomes routine but not *too* routine. You don't want your movements to become predictable (a pattern that presentation coach Olivia Mitchell characterizes as acting like a "tennis umpire" or a "lighthouse")[1]. In sum, don't overcomplicate this; just make sure you regularly maintain eye contact with people in different sections of the audience.
- **Pick out one person in each sector with whom to make eye contact during your talk.** Hold eye contact until it is reciprocated. You might even get a nod. Then move on. Be sure not to break eye contact in mid-sentence. You'd be surprised how effectively this works. A few years ago a group of friends and I attended the Broadway play *Barrymore*, starring Christopher Plummer. The play is a monologue with much of the dialogue addressed to the audience. I noted afterward how Plummer had, I believed, held eye contact with me for several seconds. My friends, who sat in different sections of the audience, said *the same thing. Everybody* thought Plummer was, at one point, looking right at them.
- **Having said the above, remember that in smaller groups, some people may be uncomfortable with eye contact.** You can tell if that's the case. Just focus on another audience member.
- **Also remember that the point of eye contact is to establish a relationship between the presenter and the audience.** We are obviously talking about a generalized relationship here, and the audience's view of that relationship is more an overall impression than a tally of how many times you looked at individuals. You can maintain an overall atmosphere of contact by looking at the audience instead of at your slides, and by looking up from your notes as much as possible.
- **In relation to the latter suggestion about notes, be sure to finish a sentence while you are looking up.** Only then should you glance downward to your notes.

5. USE PROVEN STRATEGIES TO INVITE AUDIENCE INVOLVEMENT

Audience involvement enhances listenability and your appeal as a speaker, but it is a double-edged sword. If you encourage involvement, you often wind up with a more engaged and entertained audience. However—and this is a big, mighty scary "however"—you run the risk of encouraging the subspecies of audience members who are attention junkies and want to take over the presentation. (I'll show you how to deal with them in Chapter 4, Step 6.)

Having served up that disclaimer, let me note that experience, research, and common sense demonstrate that audiences retain more and pay attention when they are involved in some fashion.

The most basic tool for encouraging participation is simply asking questions. There are several ways to ask a question, and all carry specific benefits and risks.

You can ask a question of the entire group and hope someone responds. The upside is that if you get an answer, it is likely to be responsive rather than reflexive. The downside is that if no one responds, you look a little silly, and if a boorish attention junkie responds (sometimes repeatedly), you may have to deal with disruption. One way around this is to ask for a show of hands ("How many think this approach might work? Please raise your hand") and then call on one of the hand-raisers who looks like he or she might have a lively and intelligent addition to the conversation.

Alternately, you can single out an individual. This can backfire if the target is unresponsive or takes the question as an affront. However, if you are in a position of authority over the group—say, delivering a mandatory training—this technique can be a powerful motivation for audience members to pay attention, because they know they could be next on the hot seat. I can't prove this, but I feel that subconsciously, many people *like* being put on the spot in a competitive environment and take some satisfaction in being held to task. So if you want to channel your inner Professor Kingsfield from *The Paper Chase*, give it a try if you believe your personality and the situation lend themselves to the approach.

My favored no-risk mechanism is to frame the inquiry as a rhetorical question and then call on people who respond or look as though they are going to respond. You can fake this if you want:

Me: "But the question is, how do we make this approach work?"
(Pause. If there's no response, just leave it as a rhetorical question and continue with your presentation: "One method that consistently . . .")

Or try this approach:

Me: "But the question is, how do we make this approach work?"
(Scan the room for signs of people who look like they can be made to offer a contribution.)

Me: "Wow, I see a lot of people who look like they have ideas to offer."
(The technical name we use in the business for this technique is "a lie," but remember that you can't get caught, because most members of the audience, if they are seated facing you, can't see the other members.)

Me: "And I think I saw Bob in the last row ready to contribute."
(Pick the person you think looked as though he or she had something to add. This technique allows you to read the room and move on if the audience is dead, or to select a responder in a nonthreatening way.)

There is one situation where you *don't* want to get people talking, at least right away: when you are trying to persuade them and possibly change their opinions. There is more on this in Step 9 below, but note here that people become much more intransigent once they have publicly stated an opinion. In other words, if you allow or force them to oppose you publicly in the beginning, you will *never* be able to change their views by the end.

If you do want to gauge the attitude of an audience, I have one participation tactic that usually works very well: Conduct an anonymous poll at the beginning of the presentation. Paper handouts with one or two questions work well; 3 × 5 index cards work better. If you have an audience of 50, it will only take a helper five minutes or so to tabulate the questions and maybe another five minutes to write down some of the more provocative responses. That translates to 10 minutes of your presentation, during which the audience is in some suspense waiting for the results while your helper tallies the numbers.

If you don't have a stake in the outcome of who favors what view, or even if you do and feel confident you will change some hearts and minds, conduct a poll of attitudes *at the beginning and end* of the presentation. You now have two suspense points—and I guarantee that the audience will be curious about whether attitudes changed during the presentation.

6. GET QUESTIONS ROLLING WITH A PLANT IN THE AUDIENCE

The typical peak time for audience involvement is the end of the presentation, often reserved for question-and-answer. Presenters have differing opinions on the best placement of questions; some like to have audience members ask during the session, while others prefer to have all questions posed at the end. In my experience, end-of-session questions work best with very large audiences, while smaller groups lend themselves to more interaction. The subject matter and your general level of comfort play into the optimal arrangement as well. There's no reason why you can't do both: "We'll have questions and answers at the end, but if there's something you think is important to clarify during the presentation, please feel free to ask."

But nothing short of being tarred and feathered is so demoralizing as concluding with, "And now, I'll take your questions" and not getting any. I see nothing morally wrong with having a confederate armed with a question and getting the Q and A rolling. I've actually approached a total stranger in the audience a few minutes before the beginning and asked if they would help move the session along at the end by asking the first question. I might even have proposed a question or two. This isn't falsification; you are, after all, planning a legitimate addendum to the talk, and if your plant lets out the secret, so what? You plead guilty to the crime of careful planning and move on.

7. ELIMINATE RHETORICAL FLOURISHES

You will obliterate your credibility by sounding like a caricature of a bad speaker. Don't use hackneyed, clichéd, or flowery language. Don't say these things:

- "Last but not least . . ."
- "It gives me great pleasure to . . ."
- "We are gathered here today . . ." (unless you are performing a marriage ceremony)
- "It is with a heavy heart . . ."
- "I'd like to thank the many people . . ."
- "I'd like to begin . . ." (This phrase is particularly hated by legendary public speaking teacher Reid Buckley, who advised, "Begin, damn it. Don't hem and haw."[2])

8. PROJECT LUCIDITY AND ORGANIZATION BY MONITORING TIME AND MILESTONES ALONG THE WAY TO MAINTAIN INTEREST; AVOID RUNNING LONG OR CUTTING MATERIAL SHORT

Some presentations are delivered with strict time limits. The length of others is governed only by common sense. Bearing in mind the maxim "No one ever complained that a talk was too short," keep within your limits.

Remember that if you don't keep the components of your presentation within a time frame with milestones along the way, ending on time will be like pulling the plug on a TV show that is only two-thirds complete. If you panic when you realize you have only five minutes left and try to cram everything in, you will look exactly like someone who is panicking and is trying to cram everything in.

So keep tabs on expended time by sections. If your presentation is divided up into beginning, middle, and end, take note of when each segment should conclude and adjust accordingly. If it's easier, pick three or four event milestones—perhaps an anecdote, the demonstration of a device, a particular slide projected on the screen, and the beginning of question-and-answer.

This can be difficult if there is no clock visible. It's best not to look at your watch while presenting (although there are worse things, from an audience's standpoint, than a presenter concerned with time), so you might use your phone or other device placed on the lectern. If you need only a couple of time reminders, you can set your phone to vibrate and schedule two alarms. With a little practice, you can simply reach in your pocket and end the buzzing. If you have a cohort in the audience, he or she can give you a planned, inconspicuous series of clues.

Remember, a speaker transparently cramming in material at the end loses credibility. Virtually any technique you use to keep on time-track is better than none at all. Even admitting you have a tendency to run long and assigning a member of the audience to give you reminders ("Bill, would you be sure to remind me to start questions at 10:30?") is better than a tailspin at the end.

9. WHEN TRYING TO PERSUADE, FRAME STATISTICS WITHIN STORIES—BUT DON'T MISLEAD OR OVERREACH

We dealt with the concept of using stories instead of data dumps earlier (Chapter 2, Step 2), but statistics need additional attention because of their role in enhancing—or destroying—credibility. When we think the facts are on our side, we have a tendency to believe that the numbers will somehow make the truth self-evident. That's not the case. In fact, bombarding your listeners with data may have the opposite effect. In addition to being boring and incomprehensible, you can appear downright deceptive. Most audiences know full well that statistics can be tortured into saying whatever the user wants, and when a speaker appears to abandon person-to-person common sense in favor of a numerical fusillade, listeners become skeptical.

So when you use statistics, *frame them* and *give them meaning*. Here is an example:

"About 45,000 people die in auto wrecks each year, and unfortunately that kind of tragedy is so common that we tend to tune out. But think of it this way: That's the equivalent of a fully loaded passenger jet crashing, with no survivors, every day for a year."[3]

Be careful not to misinterpret statistics or stretch their meaning beyond what can reasonably be interpreted. A correlation, for example, does not necessarily imply cause and effect. Don't do this:

"A new freeway will be good for the economy of our town. I know a lot of people here are worried about the impact of this proposed development, but let me tell

you about my friends Bill and Ellie. They live in a town the same size as ours in Monroe County, about 50 miles from here, and they opposed a similar highway there. But after the highway was built, their property values went up 25 percent."

The statistic may be true, but because one thing happened and then something happened after does not mean that the first event caused the second. Property values could have gone up for many reasons—in fact, building the road may have been a reaction to population increases in the town, and property values may have escalated simply because the locale was becoming more popular.

Be careful with statistics. To help you sort out the fine points of using stats, I have provided a 10-point guide in the Appendix.

10. ASK FOR WHAT YOU WANT

Audiences feel cheated if, at the conclusion of a presentation, they don't know exactly what it was about or, specifically, what you want from them. They might not agree with you, and they might not give you what they want, but if you don't include a specific call to action, your listeners will . . .

a. be confused and frustrated, and worse, from your perspective,
b. not give you what you want, because they don't know what it is.

Do you want their vote? Give them good reasons to vote for you, and then *ask them to do it.* Do you want them to join you in supporting a cause? Tell them why they should, and *ask them to do it.*

Do you want their help in achieving a goal? Professional speaker Brian Tracy uses this example of a call to action at the end of a speech, and explains how to introduce the call to action.

"We have great challenges and great opportunities, and with your help, we will meet them and make this next year the best year in our history!"

Imagine an exclamation point at the end of your call to action, pick up your tempo and energy as you approach it, and drive the final point home. "Regardless of whether the audience participants agree with you or are willing to do what you ask," Tracy writes, "it should be perfectly clear to them what you are requesting.[4]

Chapter 4

Maintain an Arsenal of 10 Techniques to Deflect Skepticism, Hostility, and Inattention

Presenters often have a morbid fear of hostile or indifferent audiences, and that's understandable. (Note that defusing generalized fear and anxiety relating to public speaking is a discrete topic and is addressed in Chapter 8.) But remember that it's very unlikely that they will do you any physical damage unless they have come armed with pitchforks, so keep your fears in perspective. Remember, too, that there are simple techniques that you can employ to actually turn the situation to your advantage.

Audiences in general are not your enemy. Even under the most trying of circumstances, not all members of an audience will be hostile, inattentive, biased, or dismissively skeptical. But the neutral members will look toward how you deal with the malcontents when framing their own opinion of you, your presentation, and whether they want to be persuaded to your point of view. If you handle the challenge well, you can enhance your credibility, believability, likeability, and persuasiveness.

Here are 10 techniques you can use when confronting difficult audience members.

1. BRIDGE AGENDAS: FIND WHAT YOUR AGENDA AND YOUR OPPONENT'S AGENDA HAVE IN COMMON, AND PURSUE THAT ROUTE

You'd be surprised at how often a response such as, "Yes, I under-stand," or even the hoary "I feel your pain" can drain off negative energy. Granted, you can overdo this, and you don't want to be viewed as cloy-ingly insincere—as a "handler"—but if you can convince a hostile audience member that both of you are pursuing the same goal, you can often retain the sympathy of the rest of the audience. You do this by first *acknowledging* that the audience member's concern is legitimate, articulating the *common ground* that you share, and then calling for *moving forward* by bridging and combining your agenda and the complainer's agenda.

Here's an example:

> **Question from Audience**: *"If this restructuring goes through, a lot of us are going to have to move! How am I supposed to tell my kids?"*
> **Response**: *"I know how difficult that can be, and I've been there myself." (Acknowl-edge.) "And it's not something we would want to impose on people if the situation weren't so difficult. You and I and everybody here are worried about keeping our jobs, period." (Common ground.) "No solution is going to be perfect, but if we work together on this, we have a good chance of saving everybody's job in the long run, and that's what I think we all want." (Call for moving forward with a shared agenda. And don't be baited into debating what to tell the kids.)*

2. USE THE RICOCHET QUESTION TO DIVERT A TROUBLEMAKER'S QUESTION TO SOMEONE ELSE IN THE AUDIENCE—A TECHNIQUE THAT DEFUSES HOSTILITY AND BUYS YOU TIME TO THINK

A ricochet question (where you take someone's question and refer it to others) works best in a venue where you know some of the other audi-ence members. It differs from a bounceback question, which is addressed in Step 3.

You can't always use the ricochet question, but when it's appropriate, the technique not only takes the focus off you momentarily but also increases audience involvement, and in the process it may actually produce some good discussion.

It works like this:

> **Skeptical Question**: *Our numbers each quarter keep going down. Aren't we headed for disaster?*
> **Answer**: *It's true that sales are a challenge in this economy, but some departments are holding their own or actually improving. Alyssa's department had two good*

years in a row, and she's been active in training throughout the company. What do you think, Alyssa? What are the options you can identify?

Be careful, because you don't want to anger people by putting them on the spot, and you don't want to appear to be ducking questions. But executed correctly, this technique can appease the audience and sometimes the questioner.

You can ask an audience-wide ricochet question, too.

Before I answer that, does anybody in the audience have any [thoughts, direct experience with the issue, etc.]?

3. USE THE BOUNCEBACK QUESTION TO PUT TROUBLEMAKERS ON THE DEFENSIVE

If you sense that hostile questioners or interrupters are simply intent on disruption, you can sometimes put them back on their heels by asking their names. ("Sorry, your name is … ?" or "Sorry, I missed your name.") Many hecklers are like Internet trolls and are courageous only when anonymous.

You can also simply ask them what they would do in the situation. Most won't have an answer, or if they do, it is likely to be ill-reasoned. And even if your heckler does provide a semicoherent response, you have, after all, steered the conversation back to a landscape of facts, where you presumably have an advantage.

4. KEEP AN EMERGENCY STORE OF ADDITIONAL INFORMATION TO OVERWHELM A TROUBLEMAKER

You should know in advance what areas of your presentation will be controversial, so do some more homework in those areas and hold the information in reserve. Be prepared to parry a hostile question with something like this:

I'm glad you asked, because I just recently came across a new study from the federal government showing that this type of program has achieved remarkable success …

I call these nuggets "clinchers," and if you don't have occasion to use them, you can always drop them in somehow, even if it's at the end of the question-and-answer session:

Oh, and that reminds me—before we wrap up, I should mention that on a related topic, a new study from the federal government …

5. REFRAME AND REPEAT A HOSTILE QUESTION TO YOUR ADVANTAGE

Often, a hostile question is 90 percent rant and 10 percent vague interrogative. When you confront a situation in which a questioner is slamming you with a rambling semi-question, repeat the question (*your* version of it) and give your answer. In a large group, where the audience might not be able to hear a questioner, repeating the question is a good technique regardless of the intent of the person asking.

Here's an example:

(After listening to the rant) "So, the question, as I understand it, is: How do we make sure this policy is applied fairly? As I mentioned in the opening, what we consistently try to do is to ..."

There are three tricks embedded in the technique above. First, you have subtly characterized the question as a disorganized rant ("as I understand it") and shown that you are diligently trying to unpack it; second, you note that you have already at least partially answered the question and therefore reinforce your main themes; third, you reframe the issue so that you can give the answer you want to give. Don't go too far afield, or it will appear as though you are being evasive, but you do have a right to break down what you believe the relevant issues are.

If you think it worthwhile, break down a hostile rant into two or three separate questions. This clarifies the issue and also puts the questioner and the audience on notice that you have exhaustively attempted to cover the specified ground, which gives you more justification for moving on.

Then, to move on with the presentation, say something like this:

Well, we have quite a few other people who have questions, and we've dealt with three of yours, so it's only fair we move on. I'll be glad to talk with you after ...

6. REFOCUS AUDIENCE ATTENTION TO DEFLATE A SCENE-STEALER

Attention junkies in the audience derive perverse pleasure from elbowing into someone else's presentation, either by heckling, providing unnecessarily long commentary, or asking an unreasonable number of questions.

The first thing to realize about scene-stealers is that they crave positive vibes; they are usually seeking approval from the audience and will back off if the audience turns against them.

With this in mind, the first line of defense is to let the scene-stealer blather on longer than necessary. Just bite your tongue, and wait it out.

Then thank them for their input and move on; this will often end the confrontation. But because these types have a defective off-switch, some will blindly go forth until they sense that everyone around them is becoming really uncomfortable. That's when you answer, but be sure to address *everyone,* not just the malcontent. If you talk only to the malcontent, you will encourage him or her to keep blathering.

Presentation expert Olivia Mitchell, who has an excellent video about handling hecklers, recommends that as a last resort, if nothing stops the malcontent, you ask the audience if they would rather listen to you than the heckler. It is to be hoped that they choose you, in which case your malcontent is facing disapproval—exactly the opposite of what most attention junkies crave.[1]

7. BE THE GROWNUP IN THE ROOM

Your posture and demeanor can go a long way toward defusing a troublemaker or at least luring the audience to your side of the dispute. You generally don't want to get into a shouting match with a heckler, because then you are stepping into their territory and doing battle on their terms. (I say "generally" because you may have a successful tough-guy or tough-girl style that serves you well when you give a heckler what-for. If you're confident and experienced in that approach, it might win the audience over. But it also carries the risk of making a bad situation worse.)

In most cases, then, when things get ugly, you can use one or more of these techniques:

- **Avoid a confrontational pose**. Hands on hips or finger-pointing will likely inflame the situation.
- **Kill with kindness, and remain positive**. Smiling and actually lowering the volume of your voice makes you look more like an adult and makes the heckler appear as more of a whackjob.
- **If the venue allows it, move toward the malcontent in a nonthreatening way**. This allows you to demonstrate that you are directly engaging the troublemaker and also builds audience sympathy.

8. DEFUSE PASSIVE-AGGRESSIVE HECKLERS BY EMBARRASSING THEM

Eye-rollers, smirkers, and whisperers usually don't have the nerve to disrupt openly, so they act in a subterranean manner. Such passive-aggressive behavior is, in my mind, more malignant than direct heckling, because it implies not only hostility but also disrespect.

One way to shut them down is to stop talking and stare at them. Do this for longer than you feel comfortable doing it, and the audience will become uncomfortable too—and direct its collective displeasure toward the passive-aggressive disrupter. You can crank this approach up a notch by directly calling on the malcontent, pretending (with as much sincerity as you can fake) that you thought they had asked a question but couldn't hear, or that you judged by their expression that there was something wrong— perhaps, you say with concern, they might be ill.

9. WHEN DEALING WITH A REPORTER OR SOMEONE ASSUMING THAT ROLE, FRAME YOUR ANSWERS CAREFULLY TO AVOID BEING TAKEN OUT OF CONTEXT

You have certainly been in positions where it was obvious that a person asking you questions was fishing for something that could be used against you. It might have been a journalist with a hostile agenda or a coworker looking to torpedo you later. There is no way to keep someone who wants to mischaracterize your communication from taking something out of context, but you can make it more difficult for it to occur.

Use these approaches:

- **Be wary of yes-or-no answers, especially if someone is trying to set you up to give a blanket yes-or-no answer to a silly scenario.** So, if you're asked, "Do you think everyone who disagrees with you is stupid?" don't be lured into the trap. Give a reasoned, three-sentence answer saying exactly what you want to say.
- **If you sense that you are dealing with someone on a fishing expedition for something damaging, be careful about using humor and sarcasm.** If your quote is relayed in the cold entombment of print, none of the nuance of humor will be evident.
- **Should you sense that the person asking questions is seizing on something you've just said (perhaps scribbling frantically in a notebook), be sure to continue on for a few more sentences.** Clarify your points, and leave as little room for misinterpretation as possible.

10. BREAK UP THE ROUTINE TO OVERCOME PASSIVE RESISTANCE

Bored, disengaged audiences can become sullen and passively hostile if not jolted back into their happy place. Maintain an array of techniques to recapture their attention and revitalize the presentation. Here are some ways to recover when you are losing your audience:

- **Take a long pause.** Silences command attention; we are conditioned to want them filled.
- **Tease them.** "In about a minute I'm going to show you something that is just amazing ..."
- **Inject an unplanned question-and-answer session.** "We've covered a lot of ground, so maybe we should take a minute to deal with questions I'm sure have occurred to you ..."
- **Ask the audience a question.** "What would you do?" We are conditioned to focus attention when asked a question.
- **Use my favorite refocusing technique, mentioned in Chapter 2, Step 9.** Say "in conclusion," "in summary," or "the most important point I want to leave you with."

Chapter 5

Perfect and Polish Powerful Opens and Closes

Research shows that audiences make snap decisions about people and tend to remember the opening of a presentation best. In other words, the first impression is the most important element.

In addition to providing memorability, the opening sets the tone for the whole opus, in much the same way that theme music sets the stage for a newscast or an opening vignette gives you the flavor of the upcoming situation comedy.

Research also indicates that statements featured near the end of a presentation are among the most memorable. The conclusion of the speech is where you load your "takeaway"—the overall message and impression you want to leave.

Academic types who have beards and stroke them regularly while discussing heady matters call this the "primacy/recency" effect.

Just remember that you need to have a strong start and a satisfying conclusion. It's not that difficult. Here are 10 techniques:

1. WHENEVER POSSIBLE, HAVE SOMEONE INTRODUCE YOU (WITH A SCRIPT YOU PROVIDE)

An introduction adds a bit of gravitas to your presentation. In addition, as we discussed in Chapter 2, Step 10, it relieves you of some of the duties of educating your audience about you, the topic, and its importance. Plus your presence won't be diminished if you're not the one begging for quiet or reciting housekeeping details ("and after this presentation, there will be lunch in the . . .").

But whatever you do, *don't let the person introducing you wing it.* That is a recipe for disaster—the introducer might make a hash of the intro or even forget your name. Write out bullet points for the person introducing you. It's doubtful that anyone to whom you provide a prewritten introduction will complain, and in all likelihood they will be happy to have some of their burden lifted. Have the introduction illuminate the audience as to why the topic is important and why you are qualified to discuss it. It also helps to give some personal background so the audience can begin to relate to you. But don't overdo it; long, rambling, or fulsome (look it up—it doesn't mean what you think) introductions will send you into a ditch before you even get out of the driveway.

2. DON'T START TALKING TOO SOON

Bolting out of the starting gate and babbling makes you appear nervous and unsure of yourself, and because you don't have the audience's full attention during the opening few seconds, they may not get the first few words.

So take your time. Set yourself at the lectern or whatever position you are speaking from, and take a few seconds to survey the audience. This is a very powerful technique that shows you are in control, and it also builds expectation and suspense.

3. GO EASY ON THE THANK-YOUS AND OTHER TRITE INGREDIENTS OF A TEPID OPENING

Try not to thank people at the beginning, or at least don't start giving extended thanks. Doing so is trite and uncreative. If there are people you must thank, do it *a few minutes into the presentation.* It's actually *more* appropriate to do so, and your gratitude will appear more sincere that way, because you won't give the impression that you are performing a rote task. Or, if the occasion seems to merit opening with a thank-you, do it briefly, get right to the lapel-grabber, and work in more elaborate thanks later.

Saying "hello" or "good morning" can also be an energy-sucker, because typically you will receive a mumbled chorus of unsure and unenthusiastic replies. If saying hello is your style, go for it—but it's best not to leave a space during which people wonder if they are supposed to return the greeting.

Avoid saying anything stilted and overly formal, such as, "It is my distinct pleasure to be here." It's awkward, nobody cares, and it sounds like a ritualistic statement you feel compelled to recite. Instead, do this . . .

4. GRAB THE AUDIENCE BY THE LAPELS

Sadly, in the next 18 minutes when I do our chat, four Americans that are alive will be dead from the food that they eat.

That's the opening used by Jamie Oliver in his prize-winning TED Talk, during which he raised alarms about the quality and quantity of food Americans eat. A little later in the opening, he followed with "We, the adults of the last four generations, have blessed our children with the destiny of a shorter lifespan than their own parents. Your child will live a life ten years younger than you because of the landscape of food that we've built around them. Two-thirds of this room, today, in America, are statistically overweight or obese. You lot, you're all right, but we'll get you eventually, don't worry."[1]

Do you see how much more powerful an attention-grabbing cold opening is than a variation of *thank-you-very-much-and-I'm-glad-to-be-here?* Oliver cleverly galvanized the audience and set a perfect tone for the talk, which you read in Chapter 12 and can see online (www.ted.com/talks /jamie_oliver).

The point? A **provocative statement** at the very top is one way to grab the audience. Here are some other techniques:

- **Humor**. An entire chapter of this book is dedicated to humor, but let me address it here from the standpoint of whether you should use it in an open. The short answer is that yes, humor (or an amusing anecdote) is an effective opening if (a) you have the skill to pull it off and (b) it is relevant to the presentation; ideally it will be self-deprecating, so as not to put anyone on the defensive immediately. If you are not comfortable opening with humor, as you might not be on a very formal or solemn occasion, you can always work it in a minute or so later, as Oliver did in his food warning:

  Two-thirds of this room, today, in America, are statistically overweight or obese. You lot, you're all right, but we'll get you eventually, don't worry.

  Bill Clinton used the same delayed-humor tactic in a 1993 speech before a conference of bishops, during which, for some reason, he was introduced as "Bishop Clinton." A minute or so into his talk, Clinton said,

In the last ten months, I've been called a lot of things. Nobody's called me a bishop yet. When I was about nine years old, my beloved and now deceased grandmother, who was a very wise woman, looked at me and she said, "You know, I believe you could be a preacher if you were just a little better boy."

- **Tease**. Give the listener a foretaste of what's coming, and make it intriguing. Steve Jobs opened his 2005 commencement address at Stanford with a glancing reference to his honor at being selected and then invoked the "what the . . . ?" principle with this puzzler:

I am honored to be with you today at your commencement from one of the finest universities in the world. Truth be told, I never graduated from college, and this is the closest I've ever gotten to a college graduation. Today, I want to tell you three stories from my life. That's it, no big deal—just three stories. The first story is about connecting the dots. I dropped out of Reed College after the first six months, but then stayed around as a drop-in for another eighteen months or so before I really quit. So why'd I drop out? It started before I was born.[2]

- **Quote or Statistic**. This is a versatile technique, because you can almost always readily locate something of interest to your audience. Brian Tracy uses this example of quoting from a research report:

According to a story in a recent issue of Businessweek, *there were almost 10,000,000 millionaires in America in 2013, most of them self-made.[3]*

5. WHEN YOU END YOUR PRESENTATION, MAKE SURE THERE IS A REAL ENDING

"That's all, folks" is not an ending, except in a cartoon. You want to conclude with something with a little impact, drama, wit, or motivation. While this admonition appears obvious—at least, it *should* appear obvious—think how many droning and indifferent presentations you've seen that end with "Well, time's up," "Looks like we're done," or the infamous "I don't have anything more."

If your presentation involves questions from the audience, try the technique explained in the next point.

6. IF APPROPRIATE, INSERT THE QUESTION-AND-ANSWER SESSION BEFORE THE END

Many business presentations, either in a meeting format or presented to a large group, must by their nature include Q and A. The problem with this arrangement is that the event just sort of sputters out—it's over after it becomes obvious that nobody wants it to continue.

Try saying something to this effect: "Before I wrap up, let's take some questions for about 10 minutes." This has the double benefit of letting listeners know how much time is remaining and allowing you to end your presentation with a nice, satisfying thump.

7. ENSURE THAT THERE IS A CALL TO ACTION AT OR NEAR THE END OF YOUR PRESENTATION

It's frustrating for an audience to invest time listening to you and then be left with the thought "So what's next?" (See also the "ask for what you want" advice in Chapter 3, Step 10.) If you are trying to sell a product or an idea, ask for the sale. There's always something you are trying to sell:

- **If you are accepting a sports award**, you might be selling the audience on the benefit of teamwork.
- **If you are conducting a training session** on new software, you will be selling the idea of being more productive.
- **If you are giving a sales presentation**, you are selling the benefits of the product, not the product itself.
- **If you are emceeing a retirement party**, you are selling the audience on what a great guy old Bill is and how we all hope he enjoys the next chapter of life.

So don't leave the listeners hanging. Let them know what they should do to enhance the spirit of teamwork, to move forward in their jobs, to use a new product to enhance the lives of others, or to congratulate Bill for his four decades on the sales floor.

Maybe the thing you are selling is inspiration. If so, then you need to make the next step clear in your call for action. What, specifically, can and should your listeners do?

For some calls to action, it's appropriate to have follow-up handouts available, or even products for sale on the spot. (I've given talks that mentioned a particular book I've written and have seen a few people actually disgruntled that I didn't have copies for sale on the spot. Seriously. Now I always keep a few copies for what we call "back-of-the-room sales" so that my audiences can be fully and completely gruntled.)

In short, the specific invitation will be different depending on circumstance, *but always ask the audience to do something with the information they have just absorbed.*

8. SOMEWHERE NEAR THE END, USE THE JIGSAW PUZZLE TECHNIQUE TO SHOW YOUR AUDIENCE HOW EVERYTHING FITS TOGETHER—AND VALIDATE THE EXPENDITURE OF THEIR TIME LISTENING TO YOU

You invariably will want to review the information you have presented near the end, but try to avoid referring to it as a "review." That sounds too much like cramming for a history test. Instead, hit on the main points you've made, and show how it all fits together, like pieces of a puzzle, and how the audience can therefore discover a new viewpoint or understanding.

It's easy. You can even say, "So, how does all this fit together?" Summarize the main points you've touched and show how they add up to a satisfying whole.

I've revived myself several times after cratering during some disastrously disjointed talks and lectures by using the "how does this fit together" technique. After realizing I'd rambled semicoherently, I recalled the main points and invented some reason why they all added up to something that justified an hour of my listeners' attention. You don't want to make this a habit, but I make this confession to illustrate what an effective technique it is.

In sum, people want to justify their investment of time spent listening to you. Make it easy by doing the thinking for them.

9. SOMEWHERE NEAR THE END, CIRCLE BACK BRIEFLY TO THE BEGINNING TO DEMONSTRATE THAT YOUR PRESENTATION WAS A COMPLETE, SPHERICAL GEM

This is a wonderful technique and is so simple to execute that there is never any reason not to deploy it.

Simply close your presentation, at or near the end, with a clear reference to something you addressed at the beginning. Doing so communicates the notion that the entire presentation is complete and crafted from a solid block of marble. Referring back to the beginning implies that you have "proved" your case with a complete and logical progression of ideas.

- **If you started with an anecdote**, let the audience know how the story ended, or provide some follow-up to the story.
- **If you started with a quote**, refer back to it or give another quote from the same person.
- **If nothing else, just say you are referring back to the beginning**, with something like, "I started off this discussion by promising that this new product could improve productivity, so let me tell you about one company that brought itself back from near-bankruptcy . . ."

10. YOUR LAST IMPRESSION COUNTS—SO MAKE IT A CLIMAX AND ENSURE THAT YOU GET THE APPLAUSE YOU DESERVE

You have to nail the last 15 to 30 seconds. Your situation is akin to that of a gymnast doing a floor routine. If you don't stick the ending, the entire performance is tarnished.

Remember the Steve Jobs commencement address, the opening of which was described earlier in the chapter? (And do you notice how I am referring to a the opening of the chapter in this concluding part of the chapter so I can convince you that you are getting a well-thought-out, spherical view of openings and closings?) He ended it with an emotional, provocative, and funny phrase:

Stay hungry. Stay foolish.

The concluding lines essentially communicated the idea that you should persevere even if people around you think that you are being unrealistic. This echoed other parts of the speech and pointedly reviewed the main points he'd made. How does this fit together with the rest of the advice in this chapter? Remember the jigsaw puzzle technique introduced in Step 7? Remember how I advised to make it clear how the pieces fit together, as I am doing *right now* while wrapping up this chapter and being excruciatingly clever?

Don't leave any doubt as to when your presentation is concluded. Saying "Thank you, and have a good evening" is clear but unimaginative. If you want to thank the audience, you can put the thank-you right before the closing thumper, like this:

Thank you very much for inviting me and for your kind attention, and let me conclude with one more thought about our future. I'd urge us all to remember the advice from former GE chairman Jack Welch, who advised, "Change." [Pause.] "Before you have *to."*

The perfect conclusion will be the final thump line followed immediately by spontaneous applause. If I were you, I'd opt for "planned spontaneity." If you have a friend in the audience, just let him or her know the last line and tactfully ask for (literally) a helping hand.

Chapter 6

Be Master of Your Domain: Make Visual Aids, Handouts, and Room Layouts Work for You

The setting is as important as the play, and your tools integrate with your presentation to make the whole event more memorable and impactful. There are special techniques for making the most of the room you're offered, for using handouts, props, and slides, and for integrating other media into your presentation.

Here are 10 ways to maximize the effectiveness of your tools and environment:

1. SCOPE OUT THE ROOM FOR VISIBILITY, AUDIBILITY, AND COLLEGIALITY

It's imperative to check out the room where you will be presenting. The most urgent factor is to make sure that equipment you need is present and functioning. Before you do your walk-through, make sure you have the telephone numbers of the people to contact if there is an issue. Take *nothing* for granted. Hotels are a particular sore spot with me; I can honestly estimate that half the times I have requested equipment in a hotel, it has been missing, defective, or installed incorrectly.

As soon as you can, inspect the layout of the room and determine if it is adequate. Determine whether you need to change the spot from which you are presenting. If the situation is not salvageable, move to another room if possible.

You might want to rearrange furniture yourself. Staff in meeting rooms often place tables and chairs at angles where the screen is not clearly readable. In addition, people in isolated pockets tend to chatter among themselves.

Determine if the audio setup is adequate. If you want to move around when you talk, you'll need a handheld microphone. Not all microphones, even if they are detachable, are built for handheld use, so check to make sure that you can hold it without causing a lot of handling noise. Also, most (but not all) handheld microphones are built to reject sound from the rear. This is important if you are near the speakers. When a speaker picks up the output of your microphone and your microphone then picks up the output of your speaker, the sound is amplified and reamplified until it becomes a howl known as feedback. So check your range of motion to ensure that you will not be in a position that produces this effect.

You may not even need a mic. If you have or can develop (see the next chapter) a voice that carries well, you can make the occasion more intimate by forgoing amplification altogether. People who set up meeting and speaking venues often set up a microphone reflexively, even if the room is fairly small.

Organizers may fit you with a lavalier mic, which clips to your lapel or other item of clothing. Generally these devices are paired with a small, battery-powered transmitter that clips to the back of your belt. (Note that sometimes these types of mics, and others, are used for both recording and amplification, and sometimes only for recording; if it's for recording the event, you have no choice but to use a mic.) Wireless lavalier mics are probably the best option if you need amplification, for a number of reasons:

- You don't have to stoop and crane your head closer to the mic if you are tall.
- You are not nailed to a spot directly in front of a fixed mic.
- They are very good at rejecting unwanted noise and preventing feedback.

But bear in mind that wireless lavaliers are also very good at allowing you to forget you are wearing them when you converse offstage or use the bathroom—and both are occasions you definitely do not want broadcast or recorded. Learn where the transmitter's off-switch is.

One final caveat about scoping out the room: Assess the door situation, and plan accordingly. If you anticipate that people will be coming in and out of the room and the doors have a tendency to slam shut, you are probably better off leaving them open or convincing a staff member to be on hand to shut the door gently.

Doors near the front of the room are a particular problem, because people entering or exiting might come uncomfortably close or actually walk in front of you when you are talking. When I'm confronted with this issue, I sometimes hand-letter a sign with an arrow and tape it to both sides of the offending door. It reads, "Please Use Next Door."

2. PREPARE HANDOUTS THAT AUGMENT, NOT SUPPLANT, YOUR MESSAGE

Handouts are useful—and necessary for presentations where the audience needs to take away a great deal of information. As such, a handout is an excellent vehicle for including references, detailed information, contact numbers, and a subtle sales pitch for contacting you for whatever reason you would like them to.

But try to avoid making the handouts a duplication of the material you are presenting—in particular, your slides. Doing so communicates the idea that there is no real reason to look at the presenter.

3. MANAGE HOW PEOPLE USE YOUR HANDOUTS

The key to making handouts a plus for your presentation is management of how the audience uses them. Here are some effective techniques for using handouts to strengthen the presentation and not detract from the focus on you and your slides:

- **If your handouts are summaries of material that is too dense for the presentation, say so**, and during the talk, say something like, "I know that we're getting into some complex material when we talk about the relevant regulations, so I've included an analysis in the handout. You can check it out later and call or e-mail me if you have any questions. My contact information is all there."
- **In business meetings, handouts are often essential, but they can make a hash of the event** if you have, let's say, 10 people at a conference table and they are all buried in their handouts and not paying much attention to you. Worse, people may flip ahead and start asking questions about material you haven't covered yet. Try cueing them to start and stop looking at the handout. If you need participants to check or discuss a page, channel your inner schoolteacher and say, "Let's all turn to page 6 and see how this worked out . . ." When you are finished referring to the handout, say something like,

"Let's close them, and I'll get to another section in a few minutes." Make sure to close your copy, and make sure people see you close it.

- **Consider distributing handouts after the presentation, if that approach is appropriate**, and often it is. Just tell your listeners that you'll have a collection of relevant documents, resources, and contact information available at the end.

4. MAKE POWERPOINT SLIDES VISIBLE, COMPREHENSIBLE, AND IMPACTFUL

Countless books and Web sites are dedicated to creating nifty Power-Point slides (or slides in Prezi, Keynote, Google Slides, and other presentation software programs), so I won't try to reinvent that particular wheel. You can research advanced slide-making yourself, should you choose to.

I would advise that you *don't get too deep in slide-creation*, however—at least for now. Skip the fancy software tricks; so many presentations have become virtual PowerPoint competitions that the genre is almost a joke. In fact, there are several very good comedians who riff on PowerPoint, and if you take my advice and check out videos by Don McMillan, you will get an entertaining course in what not to do when making up a slide.

You don't always need slides. If you do use them, make sure that . . .

- **The audience can see your slides**. Tiny letters and objects are the hallmarks of an amateurish, Death-by-PowerPoint presentation. How often have you seen a presentation in which, from your perspective, the slides looked like the last line of an eye chart? A good rule of thumb from Microsoft is that for every inch in height of the letter on your standard-size computer screen in full-screen mode, you get reasonable visibility at 10 feet. So a one-inch letter can be seen at 10 feet, a two-inch letter at 20 feet, and so on.[1] If you have a diagram or illustration you want to include, you'll have to judge for yourself (project it, estimate the distance of your farthest audience member, and then view it from that perspective)—but err on the side of too big and too simple.
- **The audience can understand your slides**. In general, few people will comprehend a paragraph projected on the screen. If they can indeed see it, they are likely to be distracted by you fighting for attention with the slide, and both you and the slide will lose the contest. Use short phrases instead. (The only exception to this rule is when you are designing something meant to be read close-up on a computer screen, such as an online training course, in which case you have more flexibility.) Use a simple typeface. Georgia is always a safe choice, as is Helvetica. Bullet points are okay, but don't overdo them, and don't use fancy bullet points. Complex flowcharts are generally incomprehensible and comically baffling. If there is a need for fine detail, you are much better off putting the chart in a handout.
- **The slides reinforce your message**. Slides should be more like a condiment than the main course. If you want to make the point that three-quarters of the

residents of a particular neighborhood live in poverty, look for an image that reinforces "poverty" and couple it with, perhaps, a graphic that has *only* the text "75%." A slide like that will have real impact and will add to, rather than distract from, your spoken message. I'm a fan of numbers in slides, going back to my days in print when we would endeavor to come up with number-based headlines for magazine covers—*anything* with a number. For whatever reason, a number coupled with a good visual design is arresting and commands attention. (If you don't believe me, scan the next magazine rack you see, and note how many covers feature lines like "10 Ways to Lose Weight" or "5 Secrets to Increasing Your Sales.") To further reinforce my point, do an image search for "great PowerPoint slide examples" and note how the ones that jump out at you often feature a number and an image. When there is text, it is generally short and to the point.

5. GO BEYOND STANDARD TEXT SLIDES WITH EASILY AVAILABLE ARTWORK AND VISUALS

The type of clip art that winds up in many presentations has been used so often that it's clichéd and makes the presentation seem amateurish and trite. Invest some time into researching images. You may also want to invest a little money in the process, because most images on the Web will carry a copyright of some kind, and while your chances of being nabbed are slim, it's only common decency to respect the rights of those who made the images and pay for them. But many images are free and ethically available for use; search for sites that offer images available through what is called a Creative Commons license. Read the fine print, and see what sort of attribution is expected. Many sites offer first-class (both in terms of creative content and resolution) images for a modest fee. Canva.com, one of my favorite resources for all things visual, not only offers free presentation software but also gives access to more than a million stock images, some for free, some for reasonable fees.

6. USE GRAPHICS CREATIVELY

Audiences have become so numbed by presentation software that almost any inventive approach adds appeal and memorability. For example, you might try . . .

- **Having rolling credits at the end**. Instead of thanking a list of people in your talk, prepare a roll similar to the end of a TV show, and title it "Thanks to . . ."
- **Making a title slide that looks like a book cover**. Look at covers of books that deal with the subject you're addressing, and use that approach.

- **Using a photo as a discussion point**. A presentation that I regularly give that I can almost always make work (translation: idiot-proof) is about media ethics. Instead of droning on about standards for using disturbing or provocative photos, I just project one and ask what the audience thinks. You can probably easily adapt that strategy to your subject as well.
- **Using a photo, image, or short video as a punch line for a joke**. When I teach about speaking and presenting, I warn (as I do in this book) against the type of closing that sputters out with the presenter admitting that he or she has nothing more to say. As noted earlier, if there's anything less interesting than a "that's all, folks" close, it's listening to somebody rail against a "that's all, folks" close. So I simply close the lecture by saying, "Finally, never do this," and playing a video clip of Porky Pig signing off for Looney Tunes (www .youtube.com/watch?v=gBzJGckMYO4).

7. MANAGE THE PROJECTOR AND THE TECHNOLOGY

You have to run the projector. It must not run you. Show it who's boss by following these guidelines:

- **Shut off the projector when you don't have a slide to show**. You don't need to have a visual for every point. Either turn it off or insert a black slide or a neutral background.
- **Do not look at the screen during the presentation**, unless you have to point to something specific in a diagram or image, and for the sake of all that is decent, *do not read from it*. Doing so magnifies your master/slave relationship with the projector.
- **Write your presentation first, and then create slides that reinforce your message**, and only use slides when they are necessary. Don't do the slides first and then craft a presentation to accommodate them.
- **Do not use animations, fancy transitions, or other gimmicks** just for the sake of using them.
- **Do not go overboard with using the cursor as a pointer**; it's distracting. Likewise, be sure to take your hand off the mouse when you do not intend to move the cursor, because you'll probably move it by accident.

8. CONSIDER AUDIO, VIDEO, AND OTHER MEDIA, BUT USE MEDIA IN BITE-SIZE PIECES

You can embed video directly into some newer versions of presentation software, or you can simply copy a link into your slide and click on it (assuming you have a live Internet connection). I prefer to open the video and cue it up in a separate tab, and then I simply switch tabs when it's time to show the piece. The advantage to this approach is that you can start and stop the video wherever you want, and cueing it up in advance ensures that you'll move past any commercials that may be inserted at the beginning.

A short video clip can add interest and revive flagging audience attention. Just be sure to keep it short to ensure that the audience doesn't tune out and that you don't give the impression that you are merely a projectionist. You can also use audio for great effect. (In case I ask a question and no one answers, I keep handy a sound effect of crickets chirping. It's usually almost as funny as I think it is.)

Remember not to overdo these effects. Generally, a little is just enough.

9. EXPLOIT THE POWER OF PROPS

Physical props are excellent additions to a presentation. They focus attention and add drama and are a departure from a steady diet of slides.

A good prop can become a headline. When Bill Gates was giving a speech about malaria, a disease he combats through his foundation, he opened a jar of mosquitoes and released them into the hall. While the mosquitoes weren't infected with malaria, and the best estimate is that there were only about 10 of them, the point was made, and made artfully. But be careful with dramatic props, because there is always the chance that someone might be injured trying to run from the mosquitoes, and you probably could not afford to hire Bill Gates's lawyers to defend yourself. Also, be mindful about how the prop use could backfire (as when another speaker said that Bill Gates "had released more bugs into the world").[2]

10. ENHANCE FUTURE OPPORTUNITIES WITH A LEAVE-BEHIND PIECE

If you are presenting to people you don't know and you might want them to get back to you—perhaps with offers for future business—it's a good idea to create some sort of reminder. Anything with your URL and phone number will do: a brochure, a small gift item, even a business card. In fact, it looks unprofessional not to have something in hand if an attendee asks how to get hold of you in the future.

Just be sure the piece jibes with your message. For example, when I give small presentations on the future of news, one of the academic areas I study, I often give attendees reporters' notebooks with my business card attached with a paper clip.

Chapter 7

Give Your Ideas a Strong Voice: Lower Your Pitch, Raise Your Resonance, and Amplify Your Vocal Power

Everyone can improve his or her speaking voice to some extent, and people who work diligently can sometimes develop great voices. This chapter offers 10 techniques that you can apply immediately in your quest to turn your voice into a powerful and pleasing instrument of communication.

Let me make a couple of necessary disclaimers. What follows is not a formal course in voice and speech pathology, and I am not a medical professional. (I have, however, written two textbooks dealing with broadcast announcing and addressing voice and speech improvement.) If you have a problem that you suspect is beyond the scope of this chapter, I urge you to seek the services of a board-certified ear-nose-and-throat physician and/or a certified speech/language pathologist.

I have gone this route myself. As a lecturer and audiobook narrator, I put a great deal of strain on my voice, and in recent years I've contended with occasional vocal tightness. After reading an article mentioning a local physician who specialized in performers' voice issues, I scheduled a visit and was prescribed some medicine that turned off the problem like a switch. It was an acid reflux issue, a very common but until recently almost completely undiagnosed voice problem. It's not the same as heartburn, which I never had—a factor that often led to misdiagnosis of the cause of vocal inflammation.

The moral of the story is to use these suggestions but consult a trained professional if you believe you have a medical problem or desire intensive coaching for refining your voice. Often long-standing problems that you have been unable to solve by yourself can be fixed easily by people who know what they are doing.

With that said, here is a quick and easy 10-point plan for improving the quality of your speaking voice.

1. DROP YOUR PITCH BY A THIRD TO A FIFTH, AND USE "THE STAR SPANGLED BANNER" AS A QUICK RANGEFINDER

Most people sound better if they lower their pitch slightly. This does *not* mean growling out your lowest possible note and attempting to sound like Walter Cronkite after a round of steroids. In fact, super-deep movie-trailer voices are somewhat passé today, even in television news.

What I *am* saying is that many speakers simply speak in a manner where their average pitch is too high. This results in the voice not being pleasing, especially when the voice does not have sufficient resonance and power (points addressed below). And as unfair as it may seem, an unattractive voice can absolutely mangle your message. *The Wall Street Journal* reports that recent research demonstrates that the sound of a speaker's voice matters about twice as much as the content of the speech.[1]

So, as a first step, try lowering your pitch—not in an artificial way, but simply by paying attention to your average tone and lowering it by a third or a fifth.

The musical term "third" means three spaces on a musical staff, which of course is meaningless unless you're a musician. But here's an easy way to figure it out: In "The Star Spangled Banner," the first two descending tones of "O-oh say" are a third.

The word "say" is a fifth lower than the first tone of "oh." So think about lowering your tone by about the difference between the two notes of the "oh." At the most, lower to the level of "say."

Again, do not force your voice into uncomfortable levels. You can actually damage your vocal cords by such abuse. All I'm advising is that you keep an ear on your average pitch and mindfully lower it just a little.

Also, be aware that what we perceive as a deep voice is not necessarily deep; it is often simply resonant and therefore pleasing to the ear. So ...

2. NOTE THAT THE VOICE COMES MOSTLY FROM THE HEAD, NOT THE THROAT: TRY THESE EXERCISES FOR MULTIPLYING RESONANCE

If you took the mouthpiece off a clarinet and blew through it, you would produce a weak wail, like an anemic duck call. The round and powerful sound of the instrument derives from a column of air vibrating throughout the inside of the instrument and resonating, magnifying itself in the process.

Your voice works much the same way: The sound produced by vocal cords is squeaky and miniscule (they are little flaps of tissue about a half-inch long that meet and vibrate much the same way your lips do when you produce a "raspberry" sound). The vibration is then amplified in the throat, mouth, and head.

The secret to producing a resonant voice is to develop the technique and habit of producing that "head resonance." Speech and singing teachers sometimes refer to this as "mask resonance." (The "mask" is the upper nose, eye, and forehead region: the area typically covered by a Lone Ranger–type mask.)

To evoke head resonance, try humming loudly; use the "hmmmmm" sound. You'll notice that with some practice, you can feel a buzz in your head, and with further practice, you can move that buzzing sensation around to the center of your lower forehead. That's mask resonance. Now, try humming before you speak, and see if you can create that same buzzing effect when you talk. With some practice, you will.

Some people report success in creating mask resonance if they attempt to "bounce" the voice off the roof of their mouth. You may or may not be familiar with the actor Alan Ladd, who was most noted for his role in the western *Shane,* but that was his self-taught technique. Pull up a scene from *Shane* on YouTube, and you'll notice that Ladd's voice is not particularly deep, but it is marvelously rich and powerful. That is the effect you must try to emulate with mask resonance.

You can also improve your resonance a little by slightly exaggerating your "m" and "n" sounds, especially at the end of words and sentences. Just give a little extra push to those sounds and hold them a little longer. This is a technique I use when doing audiobook narrations or voice-overs. If you want to hear this in action, visit Audible.com and search on my name. You can hear free sample narrations (teasers for the audiobooks) on each book page.

3. EMPLOY DIAPHRAGMATIC BREATHING TO IMMEDIATELY BOOST THE POWER AND QUALITY OF YOUR VOICE

A quality voice has both resonance and power. The power comes not so much from volume but instead from the firmness and steadiness of the air supply.

Professional speakers and singers by and large employ "diaphragmatic breathing" to create power and resonance. This is a very important concept but one that is largely misunderstood, so bear with me through the intricacies of this discussion.

The diaphragm is a sheet of muscle that covers the bottom of the breathing area of your chest. The movement of the diaphragm sucks air into your lungs and propels it out. Your lungs don't breathe by themselves ... they are spongy filters.

Now, every person on Earth—and as far as I know, all mammals—breathes "diaphragmatically," because there is no other option. However, the term causes confusion, because sometimes people assume it is a mechanism entirely different from "chest breathing." You simply use the diaphragm more vigorously in the type of breathing appropriate for speaking and singing.

Here is how to do it:

- **Place your hand over the solar plexus area**, an inch or two below your breastbone.
- **Take a deep breath**, deeper than normal, and feel that area expand.
- **Now push in with your hand as you speak or hum**. Just give a gentle assist with the hand pressure.
- **Once you feel (and hear) the sensation, eliminate the hand pressure and concentrate on taking deeper breaths when speaking**, expanding from the stomach area rather than the chest, and tightening the stomach to propel the air up through the vocal column.
- **You will get the sensation of support for your speech coming from a much deeper place, and of your voice being more powerful**. There is no real mystery to this: You are simply taking deeper breaths, allowing your diaphragm to expand more in a downward direction, and using more musculature to propel your voice.

4. ADOPT AN OPERA SINGER'S POSTURE TO INCREASE BREATH SUPPORT

Adding power to your voice through diaphragmatic breathing is much easier when you use correct posture. The posture taught to me by operatic baritone David Blair McCloskey—who was vocal coach to, among others, President John F. Kennedy, actor Al Pacino, and actress Ruth Gordon—is literally straightforward: Minimize any sway in your back, keep the hips tucked in, and flex your knees slightly. It's a posture favored by many opera singers and other performers.

Remember that the whole idea is to allow room for the abdomen to expand, a concept that runs contrary to our prevailing notion that a tiny waist is the key to attractiveness. The idea of diaphragmatic breathing also is in opposition to the gym-class ideal of puffing out your chest when you breathe. You should actually try to *limit* chest expansion. Put your hands on your short ribs when you take a deep breath; the ribs shouldn't expand very much. The movement and expansion should take place in the *abdomen.*

One other note: Keep your belt and other clothing loose around the waist to allow room for the abdomen to expand.

5. ELIMINATE VOICE PATTERNS

Everyone has a certain pattern of vocal inflections, but when it becomes noticeable and repetitive, it becomes a distraction and a detraction. It's hard to identify your own speech issues, but with the help of a recorder, you can often identify common annoying patterns. Here are the patterns you must seek out and destroy:

- **Uptalk**. This is the *worst of all patterns*. Uptalk—constantly ending sentences by sliding upward in pitch—packs a double whammy. First, it kills your credibility, because it makes you sound like a character from the film *Clueless*. Second, it makes your voice seem higher (because it is, at the end of each sentence), thus defeating your efforts to lower your pitch. Seriously, this is a *very bad* habit: A recent survey of 700 managers found that almost three-quarters of them found uptalk "particularly annoying" and 85 percent said it was a "clear indicator of a person's insecurity or emotional weakness."[2] When a speech habit becomes *identified as a moral defect*, it's a real problem.
- **Downtalk**. This is where you lower your pitch repeatedly at the end of every sentence and sound like a small-market newscaster. It's not as damaging to your credibility as uptalk, but all in all, it's a pattern you want to break. Change your ending patterns occasionally to ensure that your speech sounds natural and conversational.
- **Monotone**. Speaking in one pitch not only bores people, but it also gives them the impression that you are bored. Worse, it can cause physical damage to your vocal cords. Pay more attention to inflection, and make your voice rise and fall naturally. Don't imitate a top-40 disc jockey; just move the pitch around a little. Listen to patterns of actors and newscasters and attempt to adapt (but not slavishly copy) their vocal variety patterns.
- **Singsong**. This is the smarmy disc-jockey pattern, characterized by artificially wide swings in pitch. A singsong pattern makes you seem insincere. Or insane. Work for more natural variations in pitch within sentences.
- **Whininess**. You become whiny by elongating vowels and stressing words at too high a pitch: "I *tooooooooold* you this would happen!" To fix, shorten up vowels, lower pitch, and stay centered on a calm, deliberative tone.

6. ELIMINATE OTHER DISTRACTING VOCAL HABITS

Aside from speech patterns, there are other habits and tics that can detract from your listenability and credibility. Not all are easily fixed, so if you have issues that don't respond to your own efforts, I highly advise you to seek a vocal coach or a speech-language pathologist.

Among the habits you want to address are the following:

- **Breathiness**. It was cute when Marilyn Monroe did it, but it's a real credibility-killer from the podium. This may be something about which you should consult a professional. Sometimes breathiness is caused by a learned or organic failure to bring the vocal cords close together during speech. However, breathiness sometimes is a function of simply not breathing deeply enough and hence not providing enough vocal support, something you may be able to fix on your own.
- **Sloppy diction**. Be careful of dropping the *ng* sound and substituting an *n*, such as *comin'* and *goin'*. Also, don't substitute a *d* for a *th*, such as "Look at *dem.*" Other substitutions, along with problems such as stuttering, are the proper domain of a speech and language professional.
- **Accents and regionalisms**. It's up to you whether you want to eliminate voice and speech characteristics that identify you as being from a certain country or region. Accents typically are not an issue for speakers unless they provide a barrier to understanding, and regionalisms usually are not troublesome unless they invoke some underlying cultural friction—say, you work in a rural area where people seem put off by your Brooklyn inflections. I'll tell you from the start that reducing accents or regionalisms by yourself is hard, because many people simply cannot detect their own accents, even when they are recorded and played back for them. Having said that, you can make a good start at accent reduction by paying attention to pitch and stress levels within sentences. This is called "prosody," and it is often a more apparent telltale of accents and regionalisms than are pronunciations of individual words. Also, if you are a native speaker of an Asian language, it is likely you form sounds in the back of your mouth more often than most Western speakers, who place a greater emphasis on sound formation in the fronts of their mouths. You can attempt to change this simply by moving your lips more and moving the tongue closer to the front teeth when pronouncing consonant sounds (especially *n*).

7. USE PROFESSIONAL PERFORMERS' RELAXATION EXERCISES TO INCREASE FLEXIBILITY AND POWER IN THE ENTIRE VOCAL CHAIN

A tight voice is not an attractive voice, and tension in the vocal mechanism can lead to hoarseness and other vocal maladjustments. To relax the vocal mechanism, try rubbing the side of your jaw where it hinges to the skull 10 times in each direction, clockwise and counterclockwise, and then do the same with the tissue on either side of your Adam's apple. (Do this gently.) Massage the side of the neck the same way, and then use the tips of the fingers to knead underneath the jaw.

Believe it or not, much tightness in the throat is the function of tension in the tongue. Your tongue is *a lot* longer than you think and runs deep into the throat. Try extending the tongue, tensing it, and then relaxing it.

Use your fingers to bounce your jaw up and down. You won't be able to do this at first because for most of us the jaw's natural state is one of tension and it resists being moved. If you can relax it to the point where it moves freely you can considerable reduce tension in the area and free up the voice.

Try the jaw-bouncing while singing. Just sing long vocal sounds: *hah, mah, mee, mah, moo.* This is best done in private, for obvious reasons.

8. USE PROFESSIONAL PERFORMERS' BREATHING EXERCISES TO KEEP A STEADY COLUMN OF AIR SUPPORT

Breathing "from the diaphragm" helps, but in addition to having a powerful air supply, you need a *steady* supply. Try taking a deep breath, exhaling with a powerful contraction of the abdomen, and breathing out through a straw. This is an excellent exercise to teach you how to pace your exhalation. (I know it sounds silly, but trust me on this one. Being able to produce and maintain a steady flow of air does wonders not only for vocal quality but for relaxation of the vocal mechanism as well.)

A similar exercise is to make the "raspberry" sound with your lips and trying to prolong it as long as possible. This is more difficult than you expect, because you can't maintain the vibration of your lips if you blow too hard or too softly. If you have trouble making the sound in the first place, put your thumb and forefinger on the edges of your mouth and squeeze slightly. Again, the object is to provide a *steady* air flow—concentrate on prolonging the even stream of air and taking deep breaths to produce a long stream.

Do not perform this exercise in public, because you could be punched by a passerby or involuntarily institutionalized by the appropriate authorities.

9. REGULARLY PRACTICE FOR IMPROVEMENTS IN VOICE AND SPEECH

Developing a great speaking voice is like developing a muscle. You can't do it all at once, and you have to practice regularly, making gradual improvements as you go along.

I would suggest that you do the relaxation and air-column exercises once or twice a day and always do them before giving a presentation. (Warming up is important; see Step 10.)

Developing a better speaking voice is largely a matter of practice, and as everyone is equipped with a smartphone, there is no reason not to record every presentation you give and play it back, listening for areas in which you can improve. You can also simply read aloud (the speeches provided in this book's Appendix are great material) and play it back, listening for the problems identified above in this chapter and practicing correcting them.

You can always benefit from hearing or seeing yourself played back. The top presenters in the world critique their own audio and video recordings, not only to improve technique, but also to identify nascent bad habits and nip them in the bud. Seriously, you're never too old to develop a bad habit; one day, you may start developing a strange gesture or an unusual vocal phrasing. It's better to let the smartphone find out before your audience does.

10. DROP THE HABITS AND PRACTICES THAT TYPICALLY RESULT IN VOCAL ABUSE

Overuse and misuse can impair voice quality and can produce some long-lasting or permanent damage to your vocal mechanism. Just as you would not abuse any expensive piece of equipment you use in your job, you certainly don't want to do anything that will impair one of your most important professional tools.

In order to keep your vocal apparatus in good order ...

- **Don't smoke**. This sounds obvious, but smoking is a particular peril for many speakers, because the habit sometimes gives a smoker the impression that his or her voice is more resonant and relaxed after a cigarette. It may be that cigarette smoke coats the vocal cords, or perhaps the ritual of smoking produces some perception of relaxation, but in the long run, smoking produces irritation, which produces mucus, which causes throat-clearing, which causes more irritation, and the cycle can continue to the point where smoking causes, well, *death*, which is a major inconvenience. So remember than any perception of short-term gain will be outweighed by the long-term consequences.
- **Don't deliver a presentation without warming up**. Always do some easy vocalization and relaxation work before you begin.
- **Don't let yourself dry out**. Have water at hand, because when the throat dries out it, becomes more susceptible to damage, and you become hoarse more easily.

- **Don't strain if there is a microphone handy and you need it**. Use amplification when it's available and you think it's appropriate.
- **Don't scream**. Straining to make yourself heard over noise or yelling at the umpire through an entire nine innings can do a lot of damage, some of it long-lasting.
- **Don't force your voice into an unnatural register**. It is usually advisable to lower your pitch, but don't force it down unreasonably. Doing that can cause irritation and, in severe cases, vocal cord nodules and polyps.

Chapter 8

Control Stage Fright and Understand That What You Can't Control Can Work for You: Being Nervous Is Good If You Channel That Energy the Way Many Famous Performers Do

Remember this classic line? "According to most studies, people's number one fear is public speaking. Number two is death. Death is number two. Does that sound right? This means to the average person, if you go to a funeral, you're better off in the casket than doing the eulogy."

While Jerry Seinfeld might have used some poetic license, polling data actually indicates that about 40 percent of Americans fear speaking in front of an audience. Snakes were ahead in the fear factor polling, with 51 percent of the quite reasonable respondents dreading them.[1]

But when it comes to fear, snakes and public speaking are directly related, for reasons I'll explain in Step 1 below. But first, let me note that if stage fright is an issue for you, it needn't be. You can blunt stage fright pretty easily, and what you can't tamp down, you can not only learn to live with but also learn to like. Here's the complete program. Step 10 is genuinely profound and will turn around your entire attitude toward speaking in public, but don't skip ahead, because I put a great deal of effort into writing steps 1–9.

1. FIRST, REMEMBER THAT THIS IS NOT D-DAY AND YOU ARE NOT ON A HIGGINS BOAT, SO REALISTICALLY, WHAT'S THE WORST THAT COULD HAPPEN?

Recall what I said about snakes and public speaking being directly related? They're not, really; I just made that up to once again illustrate how a snappy tease opening can keep a reader's or listener's attention and to keep you from skipping right to Step 10.

No, I'm joking. They *are* related. Sort of. One interesting theory holds that humans are hardwired to fear intense scrutiny because such attention is the first indicator that we are about to be attacked by a predator. If that's true, it joins a list of human fears that have some marginal basis in reality but no immediate application to life in the modern world. For example, claustrophobia makes perfect sense if you view it as a protective device that kept early humans from getting wedged into situations where they could not escape. Fear of heights is an obvious defensive emotion with some very good logic behind it—falling to your death is almost as bad as encountering a snake—but that fear is irrational if your phobia centers on being inside tall buildings.

My point (and believe it or not, I do have one coming up) is that even though you may not have a *real consequence* to fear, the *fear you are feeling* is real—because it's wired into your psyche. It's important to emphasize this: You are not feeling a fear of public speaking because you are unbalanced but instead because you are a victim of the neural pathways of your ancestral crocodile-brain.

Some people feel this fear more acutely than others for reasons that are beyond my pay grade. However, I do know indisputably that *the first step to overcoming a fear of public speaking is to recognize and accept it*, and the second step is to remind yourself that *nothing really bad is going to happen*.

Seriously—you're giving a speech. You're not going to be struck down by sniper fire or step on a land mine.

Look at it this way. Let's assume for a moment that your worst fears about giving a presentation actually do come true:

- You freeze in terror
- You then vomit on yourself
- People in the crowd become outraged because you have wasted their time and throw rotten fruit at you
- The event goes viral on YouTube and is shown on all major network newscasts

But what *really* will happen to you? Even after all these events in sequence? You won't be injured unless the audience throws watermelons or coconuts or something similar. You can always find a different job if your boss dispenses with you because of your performance, and if you move to a part of the world where there is no Internet to shame you, the change may be refreshing.

Get it? Even if the most improbable sequence of events in your neurotic crocodile-brain does manifest itself, you will not be hurt physically, and any psychological damage can be undone over time. And as to the possibility of your worst-case scenario actually occurring, have you ever seen anything like that happen? If so, please post it, because I'd like to watch.

2. REMEMBER THAT AUDIENCES ARE POOR PERCEIVERS OF NERVOUSNESS, SO DON'T LET YOUR FEAR OF BEING SEEN AS NERVOUS TURN INTO A SELF-AMPLIFYING CYCLE

So, what are you really afraid of? Most of us do what FDR warned us not to do and succumb to the fear of fear itself, *or at least of its effects.* We're frightened that we won't be able to quell a growing anxiety and our symptoms will magnify. The more fearful we become, we worry, the more incompetent our performance will become, and the cycle will feed itself and intensify.

You can interrupt this cycle with this revelation: Audiences really can't tell if you're nervous. You may feel your knees shaking, but research shows that people watching you generally won't perceive your anxiety anywhere near the level you imagine they will.

3. ORGANIZE, AND PREPARE TO OVERCOME THE FEAR OF GETTING LOST

Probably the most realistic trepidation that speakers embrace is that they will get lost and become frozen, unable to collect themselves and move forward. This can happen, of course, but I've only seen the *grand mal* version two or three times in my life. You certainly may encounter less dramatic speed bumps, but they are not necessarily catastrophic.

I get lost from time to time, but I have a couple of techniques to cope and cover. Sometimes, if it's an informal occasion, I'll simply say, "What the hell was I talking about?" It's funny and disarming, and while I certainly wouldn't use this strategy during a eulogy, it generally breaks the tension and gets me back on track (sometimes with the help of an audience member who helpfully *does* tell me what I was talking about). I might also say, "And I'm going to shock you with an extraordinarily profound point, as soon as I can remember what it is." On other occasions, ones more formal or solemn, I'll pretend that I'm pausing for dramatic effect, look at the audience, scan my notes, and sometimes walk to the front of the stage. By this time, either I'll have remembered where I was or I'll have come up with something else to say. But people actually think I do it *on purpose.*

Again, fear of getting lost is a fear-of-fear phenomenon; it is a cycle that feeds on itself. If you arm yourself with whatever tool works for you, it's possible to break this cycle before it starts to amplify. For example, if you are speaking from notes, be careful to keep track of where you are, using whatever method works for you. Flip pages when you complete the relevant section, and don't get ahead. Or bring a red Sharpie and X out the parts you've covered. If you are ad-libbing from bullet points, try writing out the points on 3 × 5 index cards and turning the cards over when you are finished with that section.

The method doesn't really matter as long as you have a method—any method—that works for you.

4. PLAN IN ADVANCE TO SUBVERT YOUR INDIVIDUAL NAGGING WORRIES WITH YOUR OWN CUSTOM TECHNIQUES

Each of us is haunted by our private and particular performance goblins. I believe that getting lost and disoriented is the most prevalent worry, but of course there are other worries, both rational and irrational. My particular stressor is the fear of losing my notes or script. In my defense, this is not at all an irrational fear, because I am the most absent-minded human on the planet and I have left notes and scripts in bathrooms, cabs, and once in a refrigerator (along with my keys, for some reason).

My containment strategy borders on a superstitious ritual. Just like some athletes wear a particular pair of socks to a contest or take a certain route to the stadium, I stealthily plant copies of my notes behind the lectern, backstage, and anywhere I can easily access. I also print out an extra copy for my breast pocket and email a PDF to myself that I can access on my phone.

Insane? Quite likely. Effective? Absolutely. Anything you can do to lower your general level of anxiety will help your overall performance, so indulge yourself, even if it involves special socks.

5. FOCUS ON THE CONTENT, AND LET EXCELLENT MATERIAL BE YOUR SHIELD

Clearly, delivery is important (or you wouldn't feel the need to read this book), but in most situations you're likely to encounter, it is the *content* that provides the main interest to the audience.

What I'm about to tell you seems obvious, but it is more deeply meaningful than you might suspect when it comes to beating performance anxiety:

The better your content, the less you have to worry about in terms of your presentation.

Think about this precept in terms of the internal talk you might have with yourself before giving a presentation:

"I have unique, valuable, and well-organized content that I've spent many hours preparing. My listeners will benefit from this material regardless of how I do. I am a neutral conduit for material they will love. Of course, if I add to the presentation with good technique, they will love it more—so in this information transaction, I have nowhere to go but up."

That's a pretty powerful mental framework, and it produces a positive, additive cycle. The focus is now *off you* and *on the content*. Hence, if you come armed with outstanding content, you can relax and enjoy the transaction. Any anticipatory nerves you have can be abated by polishing the content—which of course makes the whole experience better for everyone and less stressful for you.

6. MEMORIZE THE FIRST TWO MINUTES TO ELIMINATE LAUNCH ANXIETY

And here is a technique that piggybacks on Step 5 above: In the opening, don't leave anything to chance. While the beginning of a presentation sets the stage for audience perception, it also determines your attitude and confidence level throughout the rest of the performance. If you get off to a shaky start, you've put the ball in the rough—and while it's possible to hit the green, it's less likely.

So make sure your tee shot is in the middle of the fairway: Get to the point where you can do the first two minutes in your sleep. Practice it 20 times over a period of a couple days. Seriously—why not? That's just an hour of prep time, and you can do it while shaving (be really careful with the hand gestures) or driving (skip the hand gestures altogether).

Knowing that you can do the first two minutes on autopilot will allay your nerves considerably before and during the presentation and will vastly improve the quality of the overall effort.

7. BREATHE LIKE A PROFESSIONAL PERFORMER—WITH THE AWARENESS THAT BREATHING FOR PERFORMANCE DOES NOT COME NATURALLY

Diaphragmatic breathing, as demonstrated in Chapter 7, steps 3 and 4, not only will enhance your speaking voice but will also considerably abate performance anxiety.

Why? First, we all know the calming effects of taking deep breaths; the practice is a staple of relaxation exercises and of disciplines such as yoga and the martial arts, which rely on a calm mind and body. But diaphragmatic breathing has a special benefit in soothing a performer's nerves, because the practice inhibits bad habits that compound cyclically and make us more nervous. For example, if you perceive that your voice is shaking, your perception of your own nervousness will make you more apprehensive, and you'll feel your voice trembling more—and the feedback loop will become additive. But if you breathe properly and provide steady support, your voice won't tremble in the first place, and you will interrupt the cycle before it starts.

Another death spiral of nervousness is talking too fast and gulping for air. The faster you talk, the harder it is to breathe, and the more you gulp for air, the faster you talk, so you can take another breath. But if you force yourself to take regular, deep, diaphragmatic breaths, you will slow yourself down automatically.

Remember, breathing for performance is not the same as what we vocal performers smugly term "vegetative breathing"—the automatic function hardwired into us to process oxygen. You have to think about performance breathing and work at it, just like you have to concentrate on practicing any skill.

8. MONITOR YOURSELF FOR NERVOUS HABITS THAT ACCELERATE UNDER PRESSURE

There's a reason why we have the phrase "nervous habit." Some mannerisms and actions appear and accelerate when we are nervous, and then they cyclically contribute to our internal perception that we are losing control of our nerves.

The best way to stem nervous habits is to have yourself videoed and make a note of what you do, and then make a note to keep track of it during a presentation.

Here are some common nervous habits to watch for:

- **Pacing**. Motion is great if you have the freedom to move around the presentation area, but monitor yourself for repetitive, caged-animal walking patterns and replace them with calm-human configurations.

- **Odd hand gestures**. Gestures are tough to monitor, because they can have different magnitudes depending on the medium and the environment. What I mean by this is that a speaker addressing a large audience has a lot more latitude for sweeping hand gestures than someone on a televised medium-shot. (I recently viewed a video by a well-known speaker who probably threw up his right hand 200 times during a 20-minute on-camera talk. What works well for him on stage, or at least is not distracting on stage, looks like a cop directing traffic when compressed into video.) So think about the appropriateness of your gestures and work on restraining them if you believe they are becoming repetitive and distracting.
- **Saying "uhhh."** This habit is never attractive to begin with and often accelerates under pressure. I wish I had better advice for you than "Don't do it," but that's the only way to stanch this habit. Just stop yourself before you say "uhhh." Anything is better than "uhhh," including—and especially—silence. You don't have to fill in every second with sounds, meaningful or otherwise. A trick that some broadcast announcers find helpful is to elongate the word before the space where you are tempted to say "uhhh." In other words, if you feel an "uhhh" coming on and you are saying "we have identified the problem," draw out the "mmm" in "problem."
- **A constantly repeated word or phrase**. You know, I don't really have to tell you about "you know," but it's worth reinforcing the concept that you don't want to lard your presentation with verbal tics. Identify phrases you nervously repeat as verbal filler, and banish them. Be particularly aware of odd phrases that you tend to say under pressure. I once heard a speaker use the term "like-a-that" (I guess as a synonym for "et cetera") for what surely seemed like 500 times in a 10-minute presentation. That odd repetitive phrase was literally all that anyone remembered from his talk.

9. REMIND YOURSELF THAT MOST AUDIENCES ARE NOT HOSTILE

It's true. I don't have a particularly charitable view of humankind, but I have come to believe that few audiences want to see a speaker fail. After all, they have an investment in the experience too. While it may be true that there are individuals in the audience who may wish you ill, it is likely that the audience will be on your side, not the disrupter's. Disabuse yourself of the notion that a presentation is a you-against-them scenario, and in the unlikely event that you do encounter hostility, use the techniques presented in Chapter 4 to come out on top and make the audience like you even more.

10. FINALLY, REMEMBER THAT FEAR IS YOUR FRIEND

Okay, here's the part I asked you not to skip to. The revelation from the next sentence will be worth the wait.

Fear is good for speakers.

It fuels nervous energy, which you can recycle into a dynamic, electric presentation.

Some of the most brilliant performers in the world have suffered from stage fright, among them Sir Laurence Olivier (who once had to *literally* be pushed onstage), Barbra Streisand, Ella Fitzgerald, and Carly Simon.

On the other hand, some people simply have placid nervous systems and don't get nervous about anything. These people typically make wonderful surgeons and jet pilots, but more often than not, they are terrible speakers.

Also, some very experienced performers in low-risk situations have pretty much done it all a thousand times before and know they have nothing to fear and essentially don't care—and they, too, are often terrible.

The best performers are the ones who still feel nerves but channel that trepidation into energy. So don't focus on completely eliminating all your fear of public speaking; that's not only impossible but actually *counterproductive*. Instead, practice channeling your nerves into energy and interrupting the cycles of nerves that turn your energy against you.

I need to close this chapter by acknowledging that truly crippling fears and phobias need professional attention. For some people, it may be the case that therapy or medication is in order. Self-medication is always risky. While a cocktail before a presentation might be helpful for many, it's a difficult habit to maintain if you are giving a 9:00 AM talk, and self-medication rituals have a habit of escalating.

Chapter 9

Harness the Energy of Humor, But Learn How to Use It Appropriately and Gracefully

Humor is a glorious condiment in a presentation, but unless you are a comedian doing an act, your humor should not be the main dish. Like most spices and sauces, too much is distasteful, and the wrong kind is unsettling and at times nauseating.

By all means use humor when you are delivering a talk, briefing, or speech! I am not trying to talk you out of it. Humor galvanizes listener interest and considerably eases tension in the room. But don't force it, and don't use humor that is inappropriate or irrelevant.

This chapter provides basic guidance on the appropriate use of humor and how to be funny.

1. REMEMBER THAT BEING FUNNY DOESN'T HAPPEN BY ACCIDENT

Being funny is hard work. Pulitzer Prize–winning humorist Dave Barry once admitted to the National Society of Newspaper Columnists that his work, which appears so effortless, is actually the calculated culmination of a grueling three-step process:

- Be funny
- Use jokes
- Incorporate the word "weasel" whenever possible[1]

Okay, that's a joke. In fact, it's a classic type of humor called a *misdirection* joke, where you are led to believe that an exhaustive and enlightening explication follows but are brought up short by a 10-word summary that includes the word "weasel," which is indeed a very funny word.

How can you incorporate misdirection and the word "weasel" into the opening for a business presentation? It's simple: *Do your research.* Just do what I just did before writing the next paragraph and google "weasel" and "business presentation." You'll get some excellent raw material:

> Let me first point out that I am cautious by nature. We want reward but have to understand the risk. My favorite comedian, Steven Wright, summed it up pretty well: "Eagles soar, but weasels don't get sucked into jet engines."[2]

To continue with advice from Dave Barry, I will note with some seriousness that he does have some thoughtful advice, and I won't gratuitously misdirect you for another two paragraphs. Barry notes that putting the funny parts into his columns is "not an inspired process" and involves investing an hour or two in creating just the opening lines for his piece. You need to build new humor on the lead, he advises, and then attempt to move the piece in unexpected directions.[3]

So don't assume that being funny is spontaneous and effortless. Professionals may make it appear effortless, because it's their business. The rest of us have to ...

- **Do our research** and unearth appropriate humor.
- **Ruthlessly edit out** any humor that doesn't fit with the tone or subject matter.
- **Draft and revise until the humor works.** (Craft several alternate versions of the remark—comedians call the versions "alts"—and see which one is most effective.)
- **Test the humor on a couple of people** to see if it is funny to others or just something that amuses you.
- **Rehearse** the humorous remark until it comes effortlessly.
- **Be sure to use the word "weasel."**

2. KNOW WHAT MAKES SOMETHING FUNNY: MISDIRECTION, INCONGRUITY, AND DISCOVERED RELATIONSHIPS

Realize from the get-go that analyzing humor is mostly guesswork and is a process that completely annihilates the joy of humor. The writer

E. B. White hit it on the head when he wrote that analyzing humor is like dissecting a frog, because few people are interested in the subject to begin with and the frog dies in the process.

But bear with me when I say that a great deal of jokes and humor (which are not necessarily the same thing, as I'll explain in the next technique) rely on *misdirection,* which I demonstrated with the opening of Step 1—leading you to believe that a pearl from an academic study is going to be laid at your feet but misdirecting you into a discourse about the word "weasel." Such misdirection highlights *incongruity*—the amusing effect of two dissimilar concepts clashing, another important element of humor.

Steven Wright has built a career out of the incongruous:

I used to work in a fire hydrant factory. You couldn't park anywhere near the place.

Right now I'm having amnesia and deja vu at the same time. I think I've forgotten this before.

How do you tell when you're out of invisible ink?

Incongruity is particularly effective when it is topical and invites the listeners to connect the dots—in other words, to form, recognize, and *discover the relationships in their own minds.* For example, George Carlin, who did a lot of comedy about social mores, had a great line about a Detroit couple "suing Campbell's soups, claiming a bowl of alphabet soup spelled out an obscene message to their children."

A couple of elements make Carlin's line work. It sounds sort of newscasty in the beginning, creating the setup for the misdirection to the absurdity. (The specificity—"a Detroit couple"—adds to this effect.) But it also draws parallels to social controversies that were simmering at the time—indecency and censorship in the media—and this makes the remark a satisfying whole that resounds with some significance when the listener puts two and two together.

3. GENERALLY, OPT FOR HUMOR OVER JOKES

I define "humor" as an aspect of an event or personality that is funny, while a joke is structured: a setup, a punch line, and an expected audience response.

For example, here's how Jerry Seinfeld reminisces about his childhood in a way that is humorous but doesn't really have a setup or a punch line: He recalls how in the 1960s, he suffered through frozen orange juice "you had to hack with a knife. It was like you were committing murder just to make juice."

The line actually came from an discussion about comedy writing, and the humor was effective because it was a natural part of the *context* of the interview (he was talking about writing a routine about food) and it was *personal*—his experiences. It's also an experience a lot of us from Seinfeld's generation can relate to. It was a natural part of the conversation, and he said it and moved on, not setting up the expectation of a punch line and a rimshot. It was more an amusing exaggeration than a joke.

Remember, a joke depends on audience reaction, which is why it's risky. If there is no reaction, the joke has failed. But humor is a relevant side journey and can be equally as funny as something with a setup and a punch line. Because it does not carry such an expectation, humor works better than jokes for most presenters.

4. GENERALLY, OPT FOR PERSONAL, RELEVANT HUMOR

Funny material in a presentation is virtually fail-safe if it is personal, completely relevant to the topic at hand, and, if possible, self-deprecating.

I can't prove it, but I believe self-deprecating humor goes over well because it gets the audience on your side—feeling sympathy for you in the literal sense of the word. "Sympathy" means identification or being in sync with. Audiences not only feel sympathy with you but also identify with similar situations in their own life.

For example, here is a foolproof joke (it has a setup and a punch line) that a former professor of mine used to open each semester's new classes. I take this description from the companion volume to this work, *Write Like a Pro.*

One of my professors when I was an undergraduate taught a large lecture class and began by taking attendance and reading the names from a roster. Some of the names were challenging, and of course many names have varying pronunciations. He invariably butchered a couple of names and asked for the correct pronunciation.

After the third act of butchery he recalled how he began his career as a television announcer, and learned that a cardinal rule of saying an unfamiliar name on the air is to first make every effort to learn the correct pronunciation, but if you can't, never hesitate before you pronounce it. If you hesitate, you'll sound wrong, even if you are right.

He then recalled the time when, as a TV reporter, he had to fill in at the last minute when the sports announcer fell ill. He was required to read, with no time to check out the pronunciations, a list of current boxing champions. He did all right with names like "Larry Holmes" and "Marvin Hagler," but when he got to lightweights, mostly international boxers with names like Sot Chitalada and Jorge Ahumada, he just barreled through and brazenly bluffed. He even added the lilt of a foreign inflection as he grew bolder.

He was pulling it off, but the camera crew dissolved into a fit of laughter when he announced a bantamweight champion as a "tough little scrapper" he phoneticized as TEET-lay Vah-CAHT-ed. He of course added a confident bit of Spanish inflection to the name, which of course was actually "Title Vacated." (Here he wrote "Title Vacated" on the chalkboard.)

He used the joke at the beginning of every semester, and sometimes in public appearances where he had to meet and address people with unfamiliar names. The joke invariably worked, or at least never failed. Even if it fizzled or most people don't get it, the joke was a relevant part of the presentation and there was a reason for it to be there—unlike the awkward and all-too-common scenario where a novice speaker suddenly inserts an irrelevant story about a horse walking into a bar.

The second reason this is a never-fail joke is because the humor is about the teller, so there's no reason for anyone to become indignant.[4]

Again, if you don't have a solid setup/punch line joke, opt for situational humor, which is generally a better choice for most speakers. Situational humor just means replaying a funny observation about your experience with the topic on which you are speaking.

I give frequent talks about the evolution of new media, with the main theme being how technology allows people to do things inexpensively that would have been prohibitively expensive or impossible just a few years ago. One of my examples is recording audio and video, and I relate how just a few years ago, I would have to visit a professional studio, stocked with hundreds of thousands of dollars' worth of equipment, to record a narration, something I can accomplish in a home studio today. I need only a spare closet, some acoustical padding, a relatively inexpensive microphone, and a standard computer.

But there are drawbacks to the home studio, I tell the audience, and I give them some insight into the process of narrating audiobooks:

Even though you can technically achieve a fully professional-sounding product in a closet padded with acoustical tile, unless you want to spend thousands on having a contractor install a soundproofed ventilation system, you're stuck with having to sweat it out and gulping for air in between takes. In the summer my closet-slash-studio is like a personal microwave oven, and by noon I'll be sitting there in my underwear, sweating, panting, and reading into the microphone, hoping I don't pass out. I wonder if that's the image the listener has when, say, they are listening to me narrate an academic history of the French and Indian War.

If this gets a laugh, which it almost always does, I add a little more:

I just hope I don't die in there. I'm not a fearful person and generally don't think about death, but I am afraid of dying in some embarrassing way. I don't want future generations to have to explain that they found me in my underwear in a padded closet, clutching a book about the French and Indian War.

This type of humor comes as a pleasant diversion, and because it is not set up like a joke, there is no expectation of a laugh and hence little risk. It also—and this is the important part—legitimately adds some perspective to the issue. Should the audience sit there stone-faced, there is no punch line left hanging in the air, and I have imparted information relevant to the topic.

5. PLAN YOUR "AD-LIBS"

An ad-lib is less risky than a structured joke, because there is no observable setup for a laugh and no awkward hang time after the punch line. Ad-libs *are* risky, though, in the sense that when you think on your feet, you may come up with material that just doesn't work.

Use ad-libs the safe way: Think up a few planned ad-libs (which clearly is as illogical and self-contradictory a term as the "mandatory option" a car salesman recently tried to talk me into, but so be it) and deploy them during your presentation.

You can probably look at the program or script for your presentation and envision situations that will arise that would lend themselves to a humorous remark. For example, I once emceed an event that had an awkward moment planned where two retirees would come to the stage and stand next to each other while they received an award. By coincidence, one was six foot six and the other an inch or so taller.

I am of medium height, and I knew in advance that the grouping would be visually odd, so I used the situation as fodder for a planned ad-lib. I decided that instead of ignoring it, I would call attention to how awkward the situation was, and observe that *I felt like I was surrounded by redwoods.*

After a beat, and a very mild laugh, I would add a misdirection line:

I meant your age, *but you're tall, too.*

6. RECOGNIZE THAT HUMOR CAN ALLOW YOU TO SAY THINGS YOU NEVER COULD GET AWAY WITH IN A SERIOUS MODE, AND USE IT ACCORDINGLY

The age joke raises an interesting point. Within boundaries, you can say things in a humorous way that would offend under different circumstances. Tread lightly in this area, especially in business-related presentations, but be aware that you do have some extra leeway when employing humor—and in situations such as retirement banquets, audiences do expect a little roasted-guest-of-honor to be on the menu.

You can make profound points with humor and make them in ways that are far more effective than a serious, humorless fulmination. Again, navigate this terrain warily, but if appropriate, remember that you do get a little insulation if you are "only kidding."

7. KEEP A FILE OF MATERIAL THAT WORKS

Keeping records will amount to 90 percent of your success in using humor. I actually made up that number, but nevertheless, the concept is important: *When a story or an ad-lib works, write it down and recycle.* Do not rely on your memory; you may think you'll be able to recall all of those gems again, but you probably won't.

Your own material is far more valuable that what you mine from a third party (more on that in the next entry), because it has already worked for you, accommodating your particular style, and has already worked before the type of audience before which you will appear.

This raises the issue of whether you'll be caught repeating humor. That's a legitimate worry if you tend to see the same audience members on different occasions, but I tend to think that people don't recall humor as well as you would suspect, and secondly, using the same joke or story twice isn't a crime. If you're caught, you can counter with a declaration that you are repeating for emphasis, because, as the Romans said, repetition is the mother of learning.

8. MINE THE VAST RESOURCES THAT WILL HELP YOU BE FUNNY

Only a few years ago, you would have to buy a book of "jokes for speakers" in order to find material or inspiration, and you might have been disappointed in the quality or usefulness of the material. Today, of course, you can use the Internet to search out humor and anecdotes of specific relevance to you.

My recommendation is to start by searching for quotes. Brainyquote .com is easily searchable and contains an ocean of material. Quotelicious .com offers material searchable in various categories, as does Quotery.com. Quotegarden.com is one of the best-organized quote sites. You can also use a general search engine for "quotes about _____" to get information relevant to your presentation. I like quotes because they give you a fallback: If you use a Mark Twain quote and no one laughs, it's his fault, not yours.

Quotes are also easy to use. You don't have to set up an elaborate story or punch line. Just say something like,

As far as dressing for success, I think Mark Twain put it best when he said, "Clothes make the man ... naked people have little or no influence on society."

Also, try searching for humorous news items relevant to your topic. Be sure to verify what you're quoting and test the accuracy against several reputable sites, especially if the material is at all controversial.

Give credit for quotes and jokes. It's only fair, and citing sources builds you up in the eyes of the audience, because it shows you've done research.

But don't just drop random humor into the presentation, or it won't be funny. The effect will be that you tried too hard.

The goal is not to simply parrot funny stuff you find on the 'net. You need to adapt the material to your style. Speaking coach Lisa B. Marshall explains how she subtly alters material to make it work for her. She keeps a file of material that, while it might not be immediately relevant, can plant a seed for discovering a personal, funny angle:

Later, when you need to create a laugh line or you need a spontaneous quip, you'll have material to draw from.

For example, a few years ago I heard Lewis Black say, "I have N'Sync and Aerosmith and Britney Spears. I have a trifecta from hell." I thought that line was very funny. I know it doesn't sound very funny out of context, but trust me, it was really funny. And besides trifecta is just one of those words that just sounds funny. Trifecta. Anyway, I wrote the line in my humor file and thought about the line from time to time—mostly when I was watching Lewis Black on the comedy channel.

Eventually that led to the creation of a line which you may remember from the better conference calls article. "A flushing toilet, a crowing rooster, and a crying baby? Did you figure it out? Yep, I once heard all those sounds on the same conference call—I felt like I had won a conference call trifecta."[5]

9. AVOID THE TYPES OF HUMOR WITH A HIGH RISK OF FAILURE

I once saw a high-ranking athletic official at a major university ding his career within weeks of being hired. During a sports banquet—a huge affair at this particular division I school—in front of a packed house, he told a joke that was tasteless, inappropriate, irrelevant, and—worst of all, from my standpoint—not remotely funny. I don't remember the joke, but I do recall that for years after the incident, he was still remembered for his crudity rather than anything he may have achieved in his actual job.

I also remember looking around the room and seeing big-money boosters, university officials, politicians, and other people that mattered cast sidelong glances at each other, silently communicating the question, "What the hell is wrong with this guy?" By and large these people were not librarians who raised orchids and cooked special meals for their cats in their spare time; many had seen the inside of more than a few locker rooms and told more than a few vulgar jokes in their time. It was not so much the attempt at humor that failed with them; it was the tone-deafness and bone-headedness of the person who delivered it.

In short, in 20 seconds he impressed many people as someone not to be trusted.

Don't be that guy. Following are some categories of humor best avoided. You may disagree with some of these contentions, and you will be quite right in your assertion that some people have pulled off such humor brilliantly. However, my point is simply that for most presenters under most circumstances, these types of humor stand a good chance of being counterproductive. Avoid ...

- **Any out-of-context, irrelevant joke with a setup and a punch line**. We've covered this before, but as the Romans said, repetition is the mother of all learning (which you may note that I helpfully repeated from earlier in this chapter). Any speech that begins with "A priest and a rabbi were in a rowboat" is destined to be the mother of all turkeys.
- **Sexual humor**. Use your judgment, but avoid this category in general. Some people are able to get away with varying degrees of ribald humor, but exercise caution if you're not an experienced speaker and you don't know your audience.
- **Political humor**, especially if it's one-sided. You may think that your audience almost entirely agrees with you, and you might be right, but you stand a good chance of making enemies of a small number of people who nevertheless can hurt you. And given the fast-drying concrete that encases today's polarized politics, they probably will.
- **In-jokes**, unless you're sure everybody will get them. Absolutely the *last* thing you want to do is to isolate part of your audience and make them feel disengaged from your presentation.
- **Racial humor, insult humor, or any other category that you know, by simply invoking common sense, will be offensive**. Yes, professional comedians can sometimes pull this off—and professional golfers can hit a drive 300 yards. Don't count on us regular folks doing either of those things.

10. EXPRESS HUMOR THROUGH OTHER MEDIA DURING YOUR PRESENTATION

If you don't think you're naturally funny ... well, you may be right. Kudos to you for recognizing that we all have individual strengths and weaknesses. But even if you don't have a compelling comedic delivery, you can still incorporate humor into a presentation.

Be creative with technology. I know of a speaker who put a collection of funny business quotes on slides that changed every 20 seconds or so; he let the slide show run automatically for 10 minutes before he took the stage. Such a technique is low-risk and can get the audience thoroughly warmed up.

Funny slides can also be used during a presentation. You can cruise the Web for examples from which you can gather inspiration. You can also easily try out slides on coworkers or friends to ascertain whether they are really funny.

Use your judgment, but if you think it will fit, consider a short, funny video. As part of a lecture class I teach dealing with social media, I feel obligated to warn students that their social media footprint is far broader than they may suspect. My personal fulminations carry minimal impact with that crowd, so I choose to show a faux-news report from the *Onion*: "Facebook, Twitter Revolutionizing How Parents Stalk Their College-Aged Kids." Have a look at it (www.youtube.com/watch?v=yu4zMvE6FH4), and you'll see why it's so effective.

Chapter 10

Master the New Media: Presenting Effectively on Skype, Podcasts, Video, and Broadcast

The evolution of digital media offers incredible opportunities for anyone who wants to present any message, in virtually any format, in pretty much any location on Earth.

If you don't investigate these media, you are shortchanging yourself. Look at it this way: suppose you are the head of your own consulting company. Until a few years ago, your dream presentation—the most prized opportunity you could imagine—might have been addressing a few hundred people at a trade show. Or, if you were lucky, appearing on a TV program and reaching hundreds of thousands, or even millions, of people in what, by definition, would be a vast, undifferentiated audience—meaning that the majority of eyeballs on you belong to people indifferent to your message and disinclined to act on it.

You may still be pursuing presentation in those venues from the 20th century, and there is nothing wrong with that. Old-school opportunities still provide you with an excellent and efficient vehicle to spread your message, and a television appearance in a local market can, depending on your target market, be a coveted opportunity. But imagine how your message could transcend time and distance if you possessed the skills to . . .

- *Create a video program to reinforce your message and show it during live presentations or integrate into small group discussions with a portable video device.*
- *Address a group of potential clients, customers, or fans via Skype or another Internet communication service.*
- *Appear regularly in videos on a YouTube channel or another video service.*
- *Speak to your audience in audio or video inserts embedded in your blog or Web site.*
- *Host your own radio program that is syndicated to a group of subscribers.*
- *Not only write your own book, but also narrate it and produce it yourself, so that your audience can listen in their cars, on the beach, or anywhere they can use a smartphone, tablet, or MP3 player.*

Now, ratchet up your expectations even further, and imagine combining traditional and new-media presentation skills into a package that allowed you to ...

- *Create a virtual personal media empire in which a portfolio of your own media businesses operates 24 hours per day, the businesses feeding one another synergistically, fueled by social media.*
- *Use that empire to make yourself a recognized expert in your particular field.*
- *Perhaps, if you enjoy speaking, get very good at it, and get that personal media empire cranking, venture out into the world of paid public speaking.*

None of these goals is unrealistic! Mastering media takes practice, trial and error, a commitment to continual research, and a little daring—but it can be done.

Here's how. Note that the following entries are longer than most of those in previous chapters, because by the nature of the subject, the instructions require more detail. While I can't provide a complete course in the technical skills necessary to undertake these projects, I can give you a foundation that will enable you to do further research. Digital skills are easier to learn than you might expect, because information, tutorials, and examples are available at the click of a mouse.

I will recommend some resources in the "For Further Reading" section at the end of this book, but bear in mind that people learn differently—a tutorial that works for me may be gibberish to you, and vice versa. The beauty of the Internet is that you can be eclectic in your choice of tutorials, and if one doesn't work for you, move on. You may also find that seeking technical instruction from a variety of sources significantly enhances your perspective and helps put information into context.

Here are the 10 steps you can take to start exploring the digital frontier:

1. USE TABLETS AND MONITORS FOR SURPRISINGLY EFFECTIVE SMALL-SCALE PRESENTATIONS

Most of this book has concerned presentations in front of fairly large groups, but if you're addressing from one to, let's say, five people, consider the flexibility of using your iPad or other tablet computer. You can show relevant pictures—of a product, perhaps—display diagrams, and even show short videos.

You can, of course, plug the tablet into standard projection machinery and use it just like the hard drive of a desktop computer. But in very small groups, displaying on the screen of the tablet (and, if appropriate, allowing the audience to interact by touching and manipulating the device) can be effective.

If you have connectivity and your audience has or will be provided tablets, you can use an app called Conference Pad to show a presentation on up to 15 iPads, iPhones, and iPod Touches.

A Google Android app called JoinMe allows tablet users to share control of a main screen.

Use your imagination when it comes to integrating technology. One of my favorite tricks to reengage a sleepy audience is to conduct a poll via their smartphones. A variety of software programs can facilitate this; just do a search on "polling software for meetings" or "polling software for presentations." You'll find a wide variety of products, some of them free.

2. PRESENT VIA SKYPE OR OTHER REMOTE VIDEO MEDIA, BUT BEWARE OF LIMITATIONS AND PITFALLS

Skype, in case you are not aware, is a video and audio conferencing tool that allows a remote participant to appear on a local screen via their webcam and an Internet hookup. Paid versions of the software allow you to include several people in the video.

There are alternatives to Skype, including an astonishingly powerful program called Google Hangouts, which is part of the Google suite of apps. Participants need a Google ID, but that's easily obtained, and if you use Gmail you already have one. Hangouts allows you to record the chat using the app. (You can record Skype, but you need a third-party application, of which there are many.)

Skype and Google Hangouts are terrific tools for anyone who is giving a presentation. You can make yourself and your message available anywhere in the world on short notice—and avoid the trauma of traffic and airports in the process.

In addition, you can often convince celebrities and other notables to appear via Skype or Hangouts. This adds luster to your performance, and if you record (with permission) their appearance while being interviewed by you, the video can be a lasting centerpiece for future performances.

But there's a downside. There is some risk involved in building a remote video appearance into your presentation, because things often go wrong. Internet connections are finicky and have a supernatural affinity for dropping out when the embarrassment and inconvenience will be maximized. Also, awkward situations occur when establishing connections; your guest may not realize the circuit is live and could be fiddling with a camera or talking to someone else when the image goes up on the screen. My advice is to ...

- **Rehearse a backup plan** in case the connection goes haywire. Plan what you will go to next and how you will resolve the situation.
- **Be very clear to guests how you will start and end their participation**. Tell them, for example, that you'll begin by saying, "Welcome! We can see and hear you. How are things at your end?"
- **If possible, establish connections before the presentation**. Keep the connection open, but don't enable the audio and video until you need it.

If you are a guest via a video service, you should set up your shot beforehand. Take a look at the image captured by your webcam, and see if there is any improvement you can make with lighting and placement. Backgrounds are important and deserve some thought. Positioning yourself, let's say, in front of a coatrack just looks weird on camera.

I have constructed a "set" for webcam appearances (Figure 10.1).

In the background there is a lighted wall to provide some depth to the picture and a design with the name of my Web site. This was not an expensive proposition. I bought a vinyl map logo and some adhesive letters and put up the background in about an hour at a cost of less than $25. A screen on which I display a newscasty motion background is just a standard TV, and I feed the loop in from a laptop computer. (You can get all sorts of moving video loops for free or very low cost via download from dozens of sites.) Behind the TV is a small uplight, available at any home-products store, that brightens the wall and keeps the background from appearing flat and one-dimensional.

Should you want to utilize broadcast-quality lighting, you can purchase very inexpensive lighting kits online and in photo stores. Opt for

Figure 10.1 A set for webcam appearances. (Courtesy of Carl Hausman)

fluorescent TV lights, which produce very little heat and use modest amounts of power. Generally, you want one light in front of you and a little to the left side, one slightly softer light in front and a little to the right, and a high light providing some illumination to the back of your head and shoulders. This backlight keeps you from fading into the background. The technique is called "three-point lighting," and with a little fiddling, you can create an excellent and flattering video-cam environment. If you have an uplight illuminating the ceiling, as in the one behind the monitor, it may be able to give you enough backlight (Figure 10.2).

As to the camera itself, a good-quality webcam is adequate for any Skype or Hangouts presentation. Other types of video cameras may produce better results for some applications (more on that follows later in this chapter), but webcam technology has come a long way in the past few years.

The main thing to remember is to use an external camera. You can get decent quality from a webcam built into a laptop, but it won't have the life or crispness of a separate unit. You don't have to spend a fortune; outstanding quality can be achieved with a camera costing about $100. An excellent choice is to get a camera that mounts on a tripod or a stalk. You can mount it in front of your computer screen, display notes or a script on the screen directly behind the camera, and use your display as a prompting device, as shown in Figure 10.2.

A step up from a Skype or Hangouts appearance is a webinar (a Web-based seminar). Webinars can be very high-tech, can accommodate many

Figure 10.2 Home video lights and monitor used as prompting device. (Courtesy of Carl Hausman)

participants—who are hooked up via computer and Internet—and can include a variety of media. Webinars are typically used for training and sometimes for motivational or entertainment programs. Sometimes they are provided free to promote a product or service, and sometimes people who take the webinar pay a fee for the training or other insights provided.

Webinar presentation is not unlike giving any presentation with slides, although slides are usually more detailed and are presented more quickly than in face-to-face encounters. It's challenging to keep attendee attention in a webinar, so many presenters use interactive devices such as polls and whiteboards. There is almost always verbal interaction between the presenter and the audience. Some webinars feature the presenter live on camera for portions of the session.

Webinar presentation is difficult, and you are well advised to use a producer to handle the technical details so you can focus on the content.

3. PREPARE PODCASTS AND OTHER AUDIO FILES FOR ASYNCHRONOUS PRESENTATION

The advance of media has blurred the definition of what exactly a "presentation" is. We can't settle that debate in these pages, but I can declare that in my personal experience, in-person audiences are being replaced, in part, by mediated listeners and viewers.

Are you in the type of job where you call meetings to announce and/
or explain developments related to your enterprise? Do you invite guest
speakers to add perspective or expert analysis? Would you be interested in
reaching that same audience, with the same material, at any time convenient for them—including when they are driving or jogging?

If so, consider distributing an audio file. The audio file is commonly known
as a "podcast," although technically a podcast is an audio file distributed
through a specific type of syndication method. (Don't worry about this; I'll
explain in a moment but use the word "podcast" generically from here on.)

Let me start with the basics. First, know that podcasts are incredibly
popular. According to the Pew Research Center, the number of Americans
who have listened to a podcast in the last month has nearly doubled since
2008, with one third of Americans 12 years of age and older having listened
to at least one podcast. In 2014, according to the most recent data I am
aware of, more than 2.6 *billion* podcasts were downloaded.[1]

Podcasts do not require a lot of expensive equipment and can be distributed for free or at a very low cost.

A podcast usually runs somewhere between five and thirty minutes long
and often, though not always, includes an interview with a guest. The audio
is recorded by the producer of the podcast, and the podcast is uploaded
to a site where it is "hosted," meaning that listeners can download it or
automatically subscribe to new installments. Listeners have programs syndicated automatically to their computers, smartphones, and MP3 devices.
An MP3 is a highly compressed audio file that, because of its small digital
size, is easy to distribute. "MP3" is an abbreviation for "Motion Picture
Experts Group Layer 3 Audio," meaning an agreed-upon method, established by a professional group, for compressing the audio. An MP3 file
hosted on a server that makes it available for subscription is actually what
makes an audio file an official "podcast." So there. Now you know.

Well-known podcast hosting firms such as SoundCloud and Libsyn are
easy to navigate and provide clear explanations of the process. You can also
find thousands of tutorials for podcast creation on the Web.

I mentioned earlier that you don't need expensive equipment, and that's
true. If you own a laptop, you can pretty much engineer the whole process for free using the built-in microphone. You can't count on audio being
recorded in one take, so you need some sort of software to allow you to
record and edit the audio. You have many options, and you probably have
software that will edit audio already installed on your computer, but I
would strongly recommend that you download a program called Audacity.
It's free, and while not the simplest program around, it is very powerful,
and you can generally find the answers to your questions about using it on
a variety of Internet forums.

Why do you need an audio editing program like Audacity? There are two reasons. First, you need some sort of software to capture the output of the microphone and turn it into the type of file you can use, and second, you need the ability to cut, paste, and mix audio to fix flubs, take out extraneous sound, improve the sound quality of what you have, and perhaps add some theme music or other audio effects.

Learning to record and edit audio is an excellent investment of time and money. What's particularly appealing about the process is that setting up your own audio studio is the first step in developing your own multimedia mini-empire, and it's not particularly expensive. If you venture beyond audio into video (the next entry), the skills you learned in editing audio will be immediately adaptable to the somewhat more complex video-editing process. Additionally, good audio is the foundation of good video. In general, people will tolerate low-quality video but will not countenance poor audio.

In terms of good quality, you can produce professional-quality audio at home with a modest investment. I produce a variety of audio presentations in a retrofitted closet (Figure 10.3), and the sound quality passes muster for even the most demanding clients.

Figure 10.3 Microphone and home studio. (Courtesy of Carl Hausman)

The microphone is, in my opinion, one of the best made, and it cost me only about $350. (If you're interested, it's a Shure SM7B, and it was the microphone used to record Michael Jackson's *Thriller* album.) The computer is a standard Mac laptop, the acoustical padding was a couple hundred dollars, the boom about $20, and I sunk another $200 or so into amplifiers and cables. That's less than a grand, total, and I can tell you with absolute certainty that the audio produced here is of better quality than that from studios where I did voice work in the pre-digital era—setups that cost hundreds of thousands of dollars.

You don't need this level of equipment for a podcast, although the added quality helps. A headset microphone designed to cancel noise works perfectly well for most applications; in addition to having a highly directional microphone close to your mouth to cancel out room noise, the headset allows you to move around freely without having to worry about maintaining a consistent distance from the microphone.

If your podcast includes interviews, you can use Skype or Google Hangouts to make the connection for free, and you won't have to bother patching a phone line into your system, but wiring in a phone is not a particularly complicated process.

Podcasting is not simple, but it's not cripplingly complex, either. Developing skills and expertise in this area is an important part of a presenter's arsenal, I believe. *The Harvard Business Review* reports that about one out of five business-to-business marketers use podcasts.[2]

4. REACH A MASSIVE AUDIENCE WITH YOUTUBE AND OTHER VIDEO SERVICES

If pressed for the most important skill a presenter needs to develop in this day and age, I'd unhesitatingly say it's *talking to a camera*. Video may never supplant in-person presentation, but it is certainly making inroads. Many of the routine talks I used to give as part of my job are now online, and the people they are inflicted upon are notified by e-mail and provided the link.

It is almost inevitable that if your job involves speaking, you will be called upon to deliver on video. Do not take this burden/opportunity lightly. The attributes of an eloquent delivery to a camera are different from those for in-person delivery, and to be perfectly candid, if you screw up your moment on the tube, it can haunt you indefinitely. Once it reaches the Internet, video lives forever as a mirror with a memory.

Having said that, the upside is huge. Your training session, motivational speech, sales pitch, or whatever has the potential to reach millions of people anywhere in the world that there is an Internet connection (which, with the increasing availability of satellite communication, is *everywhere*, including the North and South poles).

To make this more intriguing, remember that you can produce your own video for free (low-quality with a smartphone), or for a not-that-breathtaking price, you can create sound and picture that rivals what you see on television networks. Seriously. I'll tell you how toward the end of this entry.

Obviously I can't provide a complete course here, but I can offer the basics for presenting to a camera and producing video of your own. Again, you can find limitless detail by searching for print and video tutorials on the Web.

Here are the steps for successfully presenting to a camera:

- **Look directly at the camera**. I mean it. Sideways glances, dropping your eyes, or continually directing your eyes even slightly off-axis looks awkward and unprofessional. You may rightly complain that you are not a television professional, but because people *are used to seeing television professionals,* you will inevitably be compared to them in the mind of the viewer. Watch your local news anchor, and you'll notice that his or her eyes never deviate from "eye contact" with you unless there is a reason to look elsewhere. This is not a "natural" habit; you have to fix your eyes directly in the center of the lens, especially when the camera is close to you. Having said that, you don't want to glare unblinkingly like Charlie Manson. Unless you are equipped with a prompting device, you will probably need to refer to notes or a script at some point. Don't be reluctant to look down at notes. Everybody has to do that— but make as much eye contact as you can while still keeping your place. What you do *not* want to do is to have a cue card off-axis; in most cases it will be obvious that you are looking away from the lens, and your presentation will have a quality that borders on weirdness. If the camera is small enough and you feel you must have a cue card, put the card *in back* of the camera.
- **Speak slowly and steadily**. Again, viewers have become accustomed to seeing television performers deliver their lines in a regular, measured meter. Be careful of wide variations in audio, because they can cause distortion, and the loud parts are greatly magnified by the technical processing that goes on within a camera.
- **Be careful of gestures**. First, find out (if you can) what kind of shot you'll be in. If it's a head-and-shoulders close-up, your gestures won't show anyway, but broad head movements will appear manic. You have more leeway with a wider shot, but gestures will still be distracting (or worse, comical) if they are not pared down to television level. But don't try to counter this by insisting on a very wide shot. The whole idea of video is to communicate "up close and personal," to quote TV pioneer Roone Arledge, and a distant shot sabotages that effort.
- **Keep your energy level high**—not through manic motion or volume, but instead through intensity. For reasons I don't think anyone fully understands,

video is an enervating medium, meaning that it appears to drain energy from performers. What in person appears "calm and collected" on video may look "comatose."

- **Remember that with video, you are talking to one person**—not "all of you out there." Don't speak as though you are presenting to a packed house. Talk as if you are addressing a friend sitting in a chair across from you.

Here are the steps for successfully producing video:

- **Obtain and learn how to use the proper camera for your application.** I list this first because there is wide variation in cameras, and your choice will have a significant impact on how the video will be used. At the most basic level is the smartphone, which actually produces a pretty high-quality picture. The weakness of a smartphone is audio—but you can overcome this by simply purchasing a medium-quality microphone and plugging it into the input jack. A good option is a lavalier microphone, which clips onto your clothing on your upper chest, but any microphone will be better than the pickup from the phone. The second level up is a webcam. A webcam can produce a very good picture and has the distinct advantage of being plugged into your computer, enabling the video to be recorded directly on the hard drive, where it will be edited. Webcams, though, are not particularly mobile and may not be the best choice when a remote setup is needed. Another option is a stand-alone video camera. These units are easily portable, have lenses that allow you to zoom in from long distances, and usually have some sort of feature that prevents (to a degree) vibration or excessive movement from the photographer that causes the picture to shake. Video quality can be very good to excellent, depending on how much you pay; there is a wide variety in the quality (hence the price) of lenses and innards of video cameras. Generally, though, you will have to go through some extra steps to import the video into your computer for editing or posting. At the top of the line, video-quality-wise, is the digital SLR (single-lens reflex) camera. While primarily designed for taking still photos, in recent years the dramatic increase in the capability of memory chips to store data has allowed the digital SLR to record several minutes of video, and the results can be astonishing. The video not only can meet broadcast standards but in some cases will actually rival the depth and definition of motion picture film. The downside is that the zoom and focus controls are not as easy to manipulate as a standard video camera, and you must also create an external connection to export the video to your computer for editing.
- **Learn how to edit video and upload it to video-hosting services.** Editing video is a process that ranges from being moderately simple to something along the lines of recalculating the entry trajectory for *Apollo 13*. There's no way to learn it other than by practice, and there's no quick way to speed up the process, so it's time to get started. Basic video editing software comes packaged with most computers, and you can obtain serviceable apps for tablets and phones. There is plenty of downloadable free and low-cost software,

too. If you're downloading, I'd suggest starting your search at a reputable site such as CNET.com, where you can see user reviews. As for uploading, You-Tube and Vimeo are the repositories familiar to most of us, though there are others. Uploading is not particularly difficult for either site, and there are of course many tutorials available to help you.

- **Upload content that reinforces your overall message** and, if possible, links to other information you have published or to your blog or Web site (more on this later in this chapter). The type of content you post is up to you, and of course it depends on your unique reasons for presenting on video, but in general I should note that video is an excellent medium for expressing emotion but not so much for fact and detail. If nothing else, having just one video of you available online puts a human face to your spectrum of digital communication—something that may be extremely valuable to you if your job or mission involves inviting people to contract you for services or appearances. Likewise, video is invaluable (and pretty much mandatory) if you are trying to market yourself as a speaker.
- **If you are marketing yourself, monitor your direct competition to see what the rules of the game are**. Are you an entrepreneurial corporate trainer? Check out what others in the field put on their video channels. You don't have to ape their approach, but at least know what is the current coin of the realm.
- **Video marketing is becoming increasingly common in many enterprises and pursuits**. And what is common today usually becomes mandatory tomorrow. Here's what I mean: I have a son who is a very good baseball player, and I recently attended a seminar on applying for athletic scholarships and learned that coaches make many of their initial decisions by looking at the players' video sites, which are expected to show clips of them hitting, fielding, and running (usually on a football field so the coaches can see exactly how fast they run over a measured distance). I mention this to reinforce the idea that if you are debating whether you need a video presence to further your job, mission, or enterprise, you probably do. Pretty soon, all of your competition will be online, and you will be playing catch-up.

5. DEVELOP AN AREA OF EXPERTISE

The key to gaining exposure in media—legacy and "new" media—is being an expert. Under this heading, I'll tell you how to do that. In the next, I'll explain how you exploit your "expert" status to carry your message over the media.

Step one is finding the intersection of what you're good at and what you like. Enhancing an area of competency is a terrific goal, but if you really don't *like* that area, you'll likely never develop the momentum to reach expert status. Conversely, you may love giving financial advice, but if you have no head for numbers or markets, all the enthusiasm in the world won't catapult you to the front rank.

A lot of ground is covered by the overlap of those two requirements, so spend some time developing the areas in which you plan to become an expert. I would recommend three areas of expertise, all sharing a common linkage, for reasons I'll explain in a moment.

A reasonable question arises whenever anyone considers vaulting to self-proclaimed expert status: What qualifications do I need? I can't provide a categorical answer, but in general the bar is probably much lower than you suspect. For example, look at the people who write and speak about business; plenty of them don't have related degrees. Offhand, I can think of several famous business commentators who studied other pursuits in school. Suze Orman, for example, was a social work major—and a self-taught investor. Much of her self-directed learning, incidentally, was from the school of hard knocks: She lost all her money in her first investment venture.[3]

The point is that while you never want to fake any expertise, you should realize that knowledge comes from a variety of sources, including self-directed research. You can certainly find some way to make yourself an expert in a niche.

6. BECOME A RECOGNIZED AUTHORITY AND A MEDIA "GO-TO" COMMENTATOR

How, precisely do you achieve expert status? Let's say you are a human resources professional and do training and speaking but would like to move up a notch in the eyes of those in your industry. One possible approach is to develop a special interest in a critical area that is always on the industry's radar. Workplace conflict comes to mind. Why not work that into more of your training sessions? You could write an article about de-escalating conflict for a local newspaper or post one on your blog, or guest-post on someone else's blog.

Adhering to this niche-focused approach eventually leads to people coming to you, and there is a resulting snowball effect from that point onward. If an issue involving workplace conflict makes the news, a reporter who does a Web search might very well come across your name, especially if the reporter is looking for a local angle. That article or TV appearance could lead to more speaking engagements, which will increase your exposure to people in your industry, which will propel your reputation as an expert, which will result in more people calling you.

Very often, external events will create an opportunity for you; if that opportunity is in that territory encompassed by what you can do and what you like to do, pursue it. I don't want to appear cynical here. I'm certainly not saying that you want to exploit events to your benefit, but if there is some reason that your expertise is in demand, you should examine it carefully, because gaining public recognition via an existing opportunity is much easier than creating the opportunity from scratch.

Let me offer a personal example. In the early 1990s, I was doing a post-doctoral fellowship at New York University, working on a book vaguely dealing with something media-ish while teaching a large undergraduate class. Most of my time was consumed with worry about what I would do after the paid fellowship. Having no actual social life at the time, I was in my faculty office late on a Friday afternoon when a reporter from a news service called to see if any member of the faculty could comment on an event that concerned privacy and the news media.

I am being vague here because I honestly don't remember what the story was. It had something to do with reporters prying into the private life of a political figure, and as that story has recurred approximately one quadrillion times since then, you'll forgive me if my memory is hazy as to the exact cast of characters. (As an aside, here's the best definition of news I've heard: "News is the same thing happening to different people.") In any event, as I was the only faculty member there on a Friday afternoon (because the rest of the faculty were pursuing actual lives), the call was forwarded to me. I told the reporter I needed a few minutes to think about it and frantically placed phone calls to friends who actually knew what they were talking about.

Twenty minutes later I had an opinion, hastily confected but digestible. The story appeared in print, and a couple of broadcast reporters saw it the next day and called me for a follow-up. That particular story died out, but when the same thing happened to some different people again a couple of weeks later, I was vaguely blinking on the radar of those who were writing about the balance of the public's right to know versus the individual's right to privacy, and I received more phone calls.

I liked the attention, to be honest. I got busy responding to multiplying media inquiries and spent many, many hours on research, essentially because I did not want to make a fool of myself by being ill-informed in the area of my alleged expertise. Meanwhile, the clock was ticking on my fellowship, and the people who were supporting me for a year actually wanted to see some results on the book I told them I'd write.

And then it hit me. (There is hope for even the slowest learner.) I had an entire filing cabinet replete with research, anecdotes, and news clippings about privacy and the media—a nicely focused idea that would supplant the generalized "book about media" thing that I was purportedly writing.

The 400 pages of manuscript practically wrote itself, because I had all the material at hand and I had essentially formed the structure of what I wanted to say in my head, because I had been repeating it so often.

My time on the dole of my benefactor was just about over, and faculty options were few, because in the minds of search committees, I was not yet a recognized expert of the faculty variety and had not published extensively in any suitably "academic" area.

And then an editor I knew at HarperCollins, then one of the largest academic publishers in the world, called and said she had seen a quote from me somewhere about privacy and ethics and wondered if I had any interest in possibly putting together a proposal for a book about the subject. If it proved acceptable, maybe over the next year I could write the book.

A cab ride later, I was at her office with my 400-page manuscript in hand and an offer that we could skip the proposal and writing and the rest of it and go right to print. As it happened, she had a hole in the coming season's schedule and was able to publish the book within a couple of months—light-speed for the 1990s.

I can't prove that having a book scheduled to come out in the fall was solely responsible for the teaching job I landed later that month, but it couldn't have hurt.

Happily, it turns out that being an expert in ethics and privacy issues related to the news media is like being a mortician. There is always a fresh and reliable supply of business. In any event, answering that one phone call led to several more books on media ethics, many appearances on national television, an editor's post at a monthly ethics publication, an appearance before Congress, perhaps a few dozen appearances before trade and academic groups, and a full professorship at a very good university.

My self-serving memoir actually has a point here: I did not emerge from the birth canal with the idea that I would write and speak about ethics and privacy. It was a lucky opportunity that I exploited—as any good attention junkie would do. I am no philosophical genius. But the area did hold some interest for me, and I was able to stay focused and keep turning out the copy.

Honestly, if I can become a recognized expert, you can too. Given the right intersection of opportunity and interest, and some hard work, so could an ambitious rhesus monkey.

Now, to allude to the point I made earlier about having multiple areas of expertise, the eggs-in-a-basket equation applies to being a recognized expert too. One area may dry up or go fallow temporarily, either because of a dearth of external events or simply because you get bored with it. Personally, I staked out two other claims to expertise: writing and speaking techniques (one fruit of which you are currently holding in your hands) and the new economies of media businesses.

The takeaway is that you should stay focused, but stay focused in three discrete but related areas.

7. MAKE A MONUMENT TO YOUR EXPERTISE WITH A BOOK AND AUDIOBOOK

I realize that this is a book about presentation skills, but today there is no way to separate the craft of presenting from the activities that provide you with the background and opportunities to present, which is why I recommend that anyone seeking to branch out as a speaker write a book.

A book is a calling card for media and speaking opportunities. It gets you in the door. There are several reasons, some obvious and some not.

It's clear that a book is a badge of expertise. This is not to say that anyone who writes a book has a coherent message; crackpot authors are legion, but it's safe to say that *most* garden-variety crackpots don't have the time, expertise, or discipline to write a book. A book is also an easily decoded indicator of where the expert is coming from. After all, nonfiction books are designed for quick evaluation of the author and the author's message. The bio is always on the back or the flap of the book jacket, and there is always a table of contents explicitly listing the overall subject matter.

In practical terms, this means that if you want to get booked for a speech or a television show on your particular area of expertise, the process will involve a lot less friction if you have a book to sum up everything for you.

Another benefit of your book is less obvious—and I can attest to this after spending many years both as a television talk show host and producer and as an occasional guest. When you book a guest who has written a book, you are essentially *booking the book*. You are not endorsing the guest. You are saying, in effect, "This book is in the news [a self-fulfilling prophecy because the publication of a book often is news], and we are talking about the book." Get the distinction? If the guest turns out to be a whackjob and the interview goes sideways, which happens, you can always repudiate the guest, because you did not invite that person on as *just as a guest*. The guest was invited to discuss a *thing*—the *book*.

As to the book itself, at the outset you need to decide whether to pursue a traditional publisher or publish the book yourself. Traditional publishing generally carries more prestige, and as you will be working with an editor, the quality of your writing inevitably will be improved. A second set of eyes helps any author and is especially helpful to someone without a great deal of experience. Publishing houses also have in-house sales and promotional people, although increasingly authors are expected to come into the transaction with their own social media "platform." (More on that in a moment.)

The downside of traditional publishing is that it's difficult to get a book published, especially for first-time authors. Publishers want as safe a gamble as they can take, and they tend to stick with established writers. Another problem is that there is considerable lag time between conception and publication. Publishers can take months to make a decision, a contract could take another month to negotiate, and then there may be a considerable interval between completion of the manuscript and the book's appearance in print or electronic form.

Self-publishing speeds up the process considerably and frees you from having to rely on other people's decision-making and scheduling. However, some of the people with whom you deal may regard self-published books with suspicion. Sometimes there is good reason: If you have purchased books from self-published authors on Amazon and elsewhere, you know that there is a lot of semicoherent dreck out there. If your book is published in an electronic version, it enters an arena of very good books and very, *very* bad books, which is to say that no particular distinction is created by virtue of its simple existence.

You can opt to publish your own book in hard print. This used to be a breathtakingly expensive process, because before widespread adoption of digitized publishing methods, a book had to be printed in large numbers to amortize the cost of the very elaborate page layout that went into setting up the opus. Today, per-unit costs for small runs are much lower, and you can arrange to have small numbers of books spit out of the machine on demand. (This is a good option for people who speak to groups and want to have a supply in the back of the room for sale. More on this in Step 8.)

Another drawback to self-publishing in print is that you generally won't have much luck getting bookstores to carry the book.

There are variations of all these options. Some authors self-publish and then, after the book has proven profitable, sell the book to a traditional publisher. Then again, some successful mainstream authors who already have a following elect to self-publish and skip the middleman. Many self-published authors have both a print and an electronic edition—often in the belief that having an expensive print edition listed next to the cheaper electronic edition on Amazon will spur sales of the electronic edition by convincing buyers of its value.

If you have a book of short length that you believe is of interest to segments of the public, you may be better off self-publishing, as small books (say, 20,000 words) are not of much interest to commercial publishers.

The process of publishing your own book is not exceptionally difficult. Visit Amazon's Kindle Direct Publishing site at KDP.amazon.com. There are pretty clear directions on how to convert your manuscript to an e-book on the site, and if you have trouble, just do an Internet search on your question. You will need a cover for the book, composed with specific dimensions. There are literally hundreds of sites where you can design your own cover, but I can wholeheartedly recommend Canva.com. It's intuitive and cheap, and it offers a tremendous variety of art, text, and designs. I designed what I think is an excellent cover for one of my textbooks for a grand total of $1 on Canva.com.

There is a no-risk way to turn your manuscript into an audiobook. Assuming you don't want to do the narration yourself, simply go to the Audiobook Creation Exchange site at ACX.com. ACX, owned by Amazon, is sort of an online dating site where book authors can match up with narrators who also produce (meaning edit and process the audio) the audiobook.

For no fee, you can post a selection of your manuscript on the ACX site and have narrators audition for you. You can pay up front or engage a narrator for a 50/50 split of the royalties from the audiobook. This latter option means you risk nothing in the process.

I would encourage you to narrate your own audiobook, though. Don't worry if you don't sound like a professional announcer. If it's your book, you can impart an authenticity that even the most mellow-toned announcer cannot match.

I will be honest and tell you flat out that you are not likely to make much money on an audiobook or, for that matter, a self-published digital Kindle edition. However, you might get lucky—and by having an audiobook in your portfolio of media products, you create a synergy that can increase the overall impact and penetration of your message. More on this is in Step 9.

8. GET YOURSELF ON THE SPEAKING CIRCUIT

You may have bought this book because your job or business requires you to speak and you simply want to improve at a component of your overall responsibility. Or you may want to learn more about presentation techniques because you have a product, business, idea, or service you want to promote.

There's no reason why you can't combine all these goals. It is to be hoped that this book has helped you to become more skillful and comfortable with presenting, and perhaps you will move to the next plateau: that echelon where you seek out presentation gigs and, reacting to your success, people come to you with opportunities.

There are more opportunities than you might suspect. Approach receptive groups, and give them an idea of what you have to offer and, ideally, a link to a video showing you in action. Most of your early engagements will be for free, although you may receive a small honorarium or, at the very least, lunch or dinner.

Whom do you approach? There are many opportunities, but here are three areas where you might start your search:

- **Service clubs** such as Kiwanis and Rotary. These groups frequently feature speakers at their meetings and therefore need lots of speakers.
- **Industry groups**. While professional organizations often feature experts in their relevant fields, they also want speakers who can offer material complementing their offerings. For example, if you have a lively and informative presentation about conflict resolution, it's actually hard to think of a trade group that wouldn't be interested in what you have to say.
- **Classes and seminars** at local colleges and universities. I will tell you a trade secret: Many college professors would love to have guest speakers to break up their classes and give their vocal cords a break. It's a fairly easy mix-and-match process to determine what classes match with your expertise and message. Be aware that professors worry about speakers turning out to be disruptive, hateful, or weird, so do your best to reassure them that you have a reasonable message that will complement the class material. Your speaking engagement might lead to your first part-time teaching job, which is what happened to me when I addressed a friend's political science class in the 1980s. You will need a degree, probably a master's or a PhD, but occasionally a bachelor's degree, to be put on the adjunct faculty of most higher education institutions.
- **Speakers' bureaus**. These firms place speakers for a percentage of the fee, and while they are naturally inclined to engage more experienced professionals, there's no downside to searching on the topic and approaching bureaus you think might be interested in your message.

9. TIE YOUR MEDIA AUDIENCES TOGETHER SYNERGISTICALLY

Trust me on this: Mastering the synergistic chain of media is the key to getting your message across, whether it's written or—especially—when it's spoken. You want to learn how to use many different types of media, so they can cross-pollinate and form synergy.

"Synergy" is an overused word, and worse, it is often used incorrectly. It means more than components working together. In synergy, says the *Oxford English Dictionary*, "the interaction or cooperation of two or more organizations, substances, or other agents" produces "a combined effect greater than the sum of their parts."

In other words, making one plus one equal four.

That's the effect you can achieve with what I call a "portfolio" of media: different media products creating their own ecology and producing a payback to you greater than the sum of the parts. (As long as I'm on the subject of definitions, I should point out that "ecology" is often misunderstood; it is not necessarily a word connected to the environment, as it means, simply, a mixture of things that are dependent on each other so that the action or inaction of one changes the composition of the whole.)

Not to put too fine a point on this, but 15 or so years ago, your synergistic opportunities to get your message across were limited. You might have delivered some good presentations at work, and perhaps someone would have taken notice and dropped your name at a local service organization that invited you to speak. Possibly, you could have parlayed that talk into a radio or television appearance, and if you became a recognized expert, there might be a book several years down the road.

Today, you can take your presentation and adapt the content to your blog—on the same day. Then take the main thrust of the blog post and summarize it in a tweet on Twitter. If you work on building a base, the Twitter post will reach perhaps thousands of your followers—people who have become intrigued by your message from not only your blog, but also your Facebook posts, your YouTube videos, and your podcast. In turn, your video and audio develop an audience of those who follow your message. Those audiences may be different in composition, and the non-overlapping members may be driven to your other media messages.

You might also advance beyond a blog and mount a full Web site with links to your other media as well as an "opt-in" e-mail newsletter. You've seen those boxes that pop up and offer you a free report or some other item of value if you provide your e-mail address. An e-mail newsletter is a terrific way to market media products, including, perhaps, your book.

And the entire synergistic one-person media empire feeds circulation of each part of your "portfolio."

Moreover, each arm of your empire reinforces the others, allowing you to amortize your efforts. By that I mean you don't have to start each separate project from ground zero; the material from one venue—and the feedback you receive—can be honed and polished for effective use in a different medium.

Your media portfolio is critical to your presentation effectiveness, for a reason I'll explain in a moment. First, let me urge you to learn how to develop a media portfolio—to understand the new-media ecology and to acquire the technical tools to do so.

Publicity and recognition all funnel back into your presentation skills. If you are interested in revenue—and who isn't?—you may discover that the new-media cycle comes back to the same basic product that has been popular since before the days of Cicero: *speaking before a group!*

That's right. Look at any famous new-media personality, and prominent on his or her Web site will be a link called "Speaking," "Appearances," or "Book _____ for your event."

So, to segue to my final technique ...

10. PUT YOUR MOUTH WHERE THE MONEY IS: EXPLORE THE SURPRISINGLY ACCESSIBLE WORLD OF PAID PUBLIC SPEAKING

Even if making money is not the primary motivation that prompted you to buy this book, no one in my acquaintance objects to making money. Also, it's a nice way of keeping score and validating that your message indeed holds value. Finally, remember that *money for speaking is out there, and some of it might as well be yours!*

I'm not trying to sell you on anything, but it's true. People who organize events where speakers are employed are accustomed to paying them and expect to do it. Even places that don't initially offer to pay will often cough up something if you ask.

There is no need to try to extract money from everyone who is interested in hearing your message. Even speakers who command thousands per talk will squeeze in a few pro bono appearances before small, worthy groups—it's good PR, and it gives you a venue to try out new material in a low-pressure environment. However, there's no reason why you should be the only one at the head table not getting paid.

Who pays, and what do they pay for?

A surprising number of organizations book and hire speakers, including . . .

- **Business groups** holding events
- **Event organizers** (people who work for independent companies that set up events for organizations)
- **Conference organizers** (such as professional and academic associations)
- **Corporations** seeking experts in particular areas of training and development
- **Speakers' bureaus** (discussed earlier)
- **Cruise lines** (yes, there are many paid public speakers booked on cruises)

What do they want when booking a speaker? They want a number of things, only a few of which are applicable to us:

- **A famous face** to draw crowds and attention
- **Someone with pull** in the industry or profession who will be a good contact later on
- **Speakers to fill breakout sessions** at conferences
- **Trainers and teachers** who can impart relevant skills and knowledge
- **Presenters who can add a new perspective** via a topic *related* to the event

If you are a celebrity making thousands for simply showing your face and saying a few words, you probably didn't need this book in the first place, but of course I am glad you bought it. Should you be an industry bigwig, it's likely that you will appreciate but won't particularly need the honorarium that you'll receive.

Now, as to the "breakout" speaker, at large conventions and meetings, it's simply too difficult to stage events for everyone to see all at once. In fact, it may be physically impossible unless there is a football stadium nearby. So organizers provide many different presentations, and participants generally get to choose from a number of choices during the day and night.

Breakout speakers, and others who speak professionally, often are experts who provide specialized training in areas of direct interest to a group. Lawyers, for example, might provide guidance on pitfalls in hiring practices when speaking to an HR group. However, there is another approach that provides a great deal of opportunity to people who want to enter the word of paid speaking: taking expertise in one area and applying it—even in a very general sense—to the broad theme of the event.

For example, let's say there is a convention of people in some health care field. You may not know anything about health care, but that's all right. There will be thousands of people there who know all about their particular health care niche but want to learn more about how you can help them solve problems *related* to their field.

- **If you are an expert in time management**, adapt your standard speech to the health care industry, and talk about patient scheduling.
- **If you are an expert on public speaking**, provide a session on how doctors can promote their practices by addressing community groups.
- **If you are an expert on sales**, tell your audience how health care agencies can differentiate themselves and reach consumers in a competitive market.
- **If you are an expert on conflict resolution**, speak to a group about handling difficult patients.
- **If you are a comedian or just a naturally funny person** who has published a few humor pieces, give a talk on how a provider can use humor to allay patients' fears.
- **If you are an expert on social media,** you can give a talk anywhere, anytime, before any group, on "How to Use Social Media in the _____ Profession."

I could go on—an epitaph that my family threatens may be on my headstone is *"He Could Go On … and On"*—but you get the point. If you follow my advice and develop from one to three areas of expertise, you can adapt material from those areas to myriad audiences. And if you develop your own media support ecosystem, you can make money not only from your speaking but also from sales and advertising generated by your books, online courses, and clicks on your Web site.

Making money is never easy, but don't undersell yourself, and always remember that large organizations have money for speakers and trainers, they expect to spend it, and if it's in their budget, sometimes they *have* to spend it or risk losing the appropriation next year.

Let me conclude by telling you a relevant story about my first paid speaking gig. I don't like to use unattributed anecdotes, because listeners and readers suspect, with good reason, that the stories may be made up, but this one is true, and you'll soon understand why I can't use names.

I was once asked to give a talk on how to "write for the ear"—in other words, to write so that it's easily read out loud. I got the job because a person in charge of hiring speakers called a university where I taught broadcast journalism. Once again, I benefited from being the only one answering the phone late on a Friday afternoon.

After I had submitted an outline of the presentation and come up with some sample material, we agreed in principle to do it, and we began to haggle on price.

He asked me how much I wanted for the talk and the subsequent hands-on seminar, which would last for four hours. I really had no idea what to ask for, and I probably would have done it for free anyway because it would look great on my résumé, so I floated the idea of $300. He assured me that *he couldn't possibly pay that.*

I got a tad huffy. Surely, I countered, a big company could pay that much.

He got a little huffy in return, letting me know in no uncertain terms that if he paid that *little* he'd get in trouble for bringing in somebody obviously not worth the company's time.

Would I take *$1,000 total for delivering the four-hour presentation to 20 people?* I actually tried to talk him *down;* I was more than a little concerned that I couldn't possibly say anything worth that amount of money and I'd be sued.

I capitulated and delivered the presentation, which went reasonably well. As I was packing up, the organizer told me that if I went to see his administrative assistant, they could cut the check later that day.

What was not to like about that deal?

The assistant pulled a file and reviewed the particulars with me.

"That's a thousand dollars?"

I concurred.

"There were 20 people there, right?"

I didn't see the relevance, but I confirmed that fact.

"And you're being paid per person, right?"

Seeing as how my main academic specialty was ethics, I figured I should tell the truth—that it was a flat fee unrelated to the number of participants—although I admit calculating in my head how quickly after cashing the check I could disappear in a country with no extradition treaty.

That was a turning point, so to speak, because it made me realize how deep some corporate pockets are. Again, making money is never easy, and high-paying engagements are hard to come by, but *they are out there.*

Somebody has to get paid. Why not you?

Chapter 11

Ten Templates for the Types of Presentations You'll Commonly Encounter

Below are 10 templates for typical scenarios you will encounter when presenting. They are in no particular order, except for the fact that related templates (such as "Presenting an Award" and "Receiving an Award") are adjoining. Also, I have put "Keynote" at the end because it is, in many ways, a combination of all other types of structures and techniques.

I clearly can't provide a universal structure for all presentations, but I believe the following entries will give you versatile guidance on structure, content, and sequence for the varieties of presentations you'll regularly encounter.

1. A TRAINING PRESENTATION

✓ Begin with a success story illustrating what benefit the members of the audience will receive from knowing whatever you are describing. It doesn't have to be earth-shattering—just an example of how learning the material being covered made it easier to accomplish something worthwhile.

✓ State what the participants will learn and how they will learn it.

✓ Again, reinforce why the material is useful and important as you demonstrate or discuss.

✓ If you are demonstrating, before each example clearly describe what will be done and what will be accomplished.

✓ If you use handouts, be sure to instruct the audience on when to refer to them and when to stop referring to them ("Okay, let's turn our attention back to …").

✓ Make sure you hit on the important points you promised in the beginning. Keep things moving; trainings are particularly vulnerable to being hijacked by getting lost in the weeds of one aspect. And trainings are especially vulnerable to negative evaluations of the process when you run out of time. After all, if your goal is to cover how to do something and you only cover half of it, by definition you have failed.

✓ Be sure to include question-and-answer, but build it into the end. Don't put it right at the end. Otherwise, if there are no questions, the training will peter out embarrassingly. Say, "Before I wrap up, let me address any questions you may have …"

✓ Close with an affirmation about what audience members can and should do now with the information and skill they have gained.

2. INTRODUCING A SPEAKER

✓ Begin by answering the question surely on the audience's collective mind: Why should we listen to this speaker? Do not begin by rattling off qualifications. Be specific as to why this speaker is apropos for this event.

✓ Give the full name and title clearly, even if you think most of the audience knows the person. There may, for example, be a journalist or visitor in the audience who will be puzzled if the introduction is not complete.

✓ Ask a question or tell a story soon after you begin the introduction. "How can you turn around a school system when there is just no money and no political will to provide any money? Our guest faced that issue in 2016, when she …"

✓ Qualifications are important, but don't overdo, and don't ramble. If the person is famous or very well known to the group, look for unusual aspects of the person's background to highlight.

✓ Never say, "This person needs no introduction." This cliché is so old that it belches dust, and it also produces some bizarre cognitive dissonance by calling into question your role in standing in front of the audience and making an introduction.

✓ Determine whether you want applause when you bring the speaker to the lectern. Applause would be out of place in some situations, such as a corporate training or the introduction of a person who is there to relay bad news. But applause is welcome and expected for most larger convocations. If you don't want or expect applause, just hand over the presentation: "Dr. Kelly, please tell us about the project." If you do want applause, be sure to cue it clearly: "And please join me in welcoming Dr. Kelly." Clap *your own hands* just to be sure everybody gets the message. It is a terrible start to a presentation to get scattered and tentative clapping in isolated pockets.

✓ Stay in place for a moment while the speaker gets settled. You may need to adjust a mic, help with equipment, or, as happens, pick up papers that get dropped in the transition.

3. A BRIEF STATEMENT BEFORE A GOVERNING BODY, SCHOOL BOARD, OR OTHER TYPE OF GROUP THAT IS HEARING OPINION PRIOR TO RENDERING A DECISION

✓ Clearly state who you are and what your interest is. Public bodies, in particular, are often very suspicious of the interests of those who appear before them and may be worried—often with justification—that the person represents some subterranean special interest.

✓ Say why you are qualified to weigh in. Do not trumpet qualifications; simply explain why your opinion is valuable, even if it is just to say, "I've lived in the neighborhood for 20 years, and ..."

✓ Be prepared to tick off three main points—a good target for a brief statement. If you like, state in advance that you have three main things to say, and count them off.

✓ Be clear at the end what it is you are asking for. Vote against or for the issue? Appropriate more money?

✓ Before breaking off the encounter, make it clear—either by what you say or your body language—that you are prepared to answer any questions. Sitting down right after you stop talking might deprive you of a follow-up opportunity, though conversely it may spare you a hostile response or inquiry. In most cases you do want to take questions, because it extends your time and influence.

4. A SALES PITCH OR OTHER PERSUASIVE PRESENTATION

✓ Open with as riveting an attention-getter as you can manage. Any sort of persuasive communication hinges on capturing and maintaining audience attention. When Steve Jobs introduced the iPhone to an audience of decision-makers—some of them skeptical—at MacWorld, he began by saying, "We're gonna make some history together today." Think along those lines.

✓ State the problem that you are going to solve. Give examples. It is absolutely essential that you phrase your pitch in terms of a solution to a problem.

✓ Go through perhaps four or five main points, being sure to show how those points are benefits—and how those benefits are part of an overall solution to a problem.

✓ After each point, somehow address and counter objections. You don't have to elaborate, but you could note, for example, "Some people have said the solution is too expensive, but when you run the numbers, the cold, hard realization is that this will save money in the long run—and we're not talking about that long a period of time, either."

✓ Include some evidence to reinforce each point—a statistic, an anecdote, or a quote.

✓ Wrap up with an appeal to logic. Review what you've said, and demonstrate how your result—what you want the audience to do—inevitably flows from the logical conclusions of your arguments.

✓ End with a clear call to action—what you want people to do, right now.

5. PRESENTING AN AWARD

✓ Always start with the recipient seated or at least *not* at the lectern. You don't want the recipient to feel like an inanimate object as you describe him or her.

✓ Be clear at the outset what the award is for—not just the particulars of the award criteria, but also the reasoning behind the creation of the award.

✓ Talk for a couple minutes about the nature of the award without mentioning the recipient's name—even if it is in the program. Build up the illusion of suspense.

✓ Announce the name of the winner. Don't bring the person up yet. Work out in advance the cue you will use to actually invite the recipient to the lectern. It doesn't have to be top-secret; "Joe, come on up" will work fine.

✓ After you announce the name of the winner, talk for whatever time you deem appropriate, providing details about the person.

✓ Be clear how the accomplishments of the recipient jibe with the award.

✓ Tell stories about the person and the history of the award. This is one of the occasions where you are expected to relate anecdotes, and barring the unlikely occasion where the award is for survival of a massacre or something like that, humor is appreciated.

✓ If you have the touch for it and you believe the recipient and the audience are in the mood for it, a little gentle humor at the recipient's expense adds to the atmosphere. Don't go full-bore Don Rickles, but an occasional jibe, well told, can heighten the humanity of the person achieving the honor.

✓ About four-fifths of the way through your introduction, call the person up. It is important at this point that you reserve some time for physically handing over the award, if there is a plaque, trophy, certificate, or other physical manifestation.

✓ Allow time for pictures when you hand over the award. Always face front and keep the award visible.

✓ You can set the award down, leave it in the hands of the recipient, or (if you are at a speaker's table) put it where the person is sitting, but whatever you do, plan your action in advance, and stick to it. You don't want two people tugging at the award or the recipient clearly wondering what to do with it.

✓ Have a line or two to say while you are both standing. It adds to the dignity of the event and allows time for the recipient to enjoy the honor (and for people to take pictures).

6. RECEIVING AN AWARD

✓ Open with a statement of what the award means to you and why. There's nothing wrong with starting with thanks, but thanks can have more impact when they are delayed and clearly not reflexive.

✓ Clearly you will have to thank people, but if possible list individuals in groups. Tell a story and thank the members of the relevant group. Tell another story and thank the members of the relevant group.

✓ Have a list of people you want to thank, and put some thought into its construction. You don't want to create enemies inadvertently by thanking some people and forgetting others. This is a difficult task, somewhat akin to the ring of people you would invite to a party. You can invite people from work, for example, but if you invite ten people from work and one from the neighborhood, there may be hard feelings among the neighbors. If you invited only people from work, it's less likely that such resentment would surface. It's better to not thank entire rings than to thank one member of a ring and not others.

✓ Try not to run long. Receiving an award is a heady experience and can degenerate into a head-trip if you don't keep organized. Seriously—look at Academy Award acceptance speeches, renowned for their self-absorption and incoherency. These are people who are experienced at being in the public eye. If they can derail, so can you. Stay on track.

✓ If there are multiple award winners and a schedule to keep, be brief and memorable.

✓ Tell stories about the organization that is giving you the award—your history with it and the people who are involved with it. That's what the audience wants to hear. Be humble. Talk about others.

✓ Conclude, if you can, with a story that wraps everything together: the people who nominated you, the organization, and so forth.

7. DELIVERING BAD NEWS

✓ Open your presentation with a straightforward statement about the bad news—layoffs, closings, whatever. You can certainly add your argument that all is not doom and gloom, but trying to bury the lead is amateurish.

✓ Read your presentation, or at least ad-lib it from a detailed statement. This is important because you may be called on to back up specific claims, or people may misinterpret, accidentally or deliberately, what you say.

✓ When the bad news is delivered, turn the focus on the positive, if there is any. This must not be done to obscure or divert. The goal should be to propose a solution-oriented path forward.

✓ Deliver your presentation in a level, steady tone. It's easy to become emotional in times of stress, but you want to be seen as collected and empathetic at the same time.

✓ If question-and-answer is involved, you are obligated to listen and show empathy. Don't obviously "handle" people with cloying remarks about how you feel their pain, but do demonstrate that you understand their concerns.

✓ Plan in advance some ending cue. You don't want to evade questions, but difficult situations can turn into pointless grinds if there is no exit strategy. You might announce that you'll take questions for 10 minutes; stick to the timetable. One way to reinforce the notion that you have to end the discussion is to have an ally fetch you and inform you that it's time to go.

8. MOTIVATING A GROUP

✓ Always begin with a story that demonstrates the situation you want the group to overcome, or a solution that you want the group to aspire to. Remember, this is different from a persuasive speech, in that you are spending less time convincing and more time cajoling to action.

✓ Try for four or five main points, depending on the length of your presentation. Keep your points congruent with the theme that you want the audience to aspire to.

✓ Use bullet points, and ad-lib. Motivational speeches read from scripts are very hard to deliver with the appropriate passion.

✓ Under each main point, include a teaser for the next. For example, if your presentation is "You Can Run a Marathon No Matter What Your Age," Main Point #1 is "You can prepare physically and feel better in the process," and Main Point #2 is "You can prepare emotionally and become calmer and more confident in the process," be sure that at some point in your discussion of Point #1, you say something like, "After the first two weeks, you'll find yourself taking stairs two at a time and not caring how close the parking space is to the store. Not only that, but you're going to view the world around you in new ways, too, and I'll get to that in a moment." Motivational presentations, by their nature, lead to a main culminating point, and a sense of internal flow is vital.

✓ Have a solid conclusion. Deliver it with impact, and then get off or move on to the next point. Avoid anything—including question-and-answer sessions—that allows the energy to drain from the room. Finish with something memorable and actionable that sums up what you want the audience to take away. Like this (you'll recognize it at the end and can see the whole speech in the next chapter): "It is in vain, sir, to extenuate the matter. Gentlemen may cry, Peace, Peace, but there is no peace. The war is actually begun! The next gale that sweeps from the north will bring to our ears the clash of resounding arms! Our brethren are already in the field! Why stand we here idle? What is it that gentlemen wish? What would they have? Is life so dear, or peace so sweet, as to be purchased at the price of chains and slavery? Forbid it, Almighty God! I know not what course others may take; but as for me, give me liberty or give me death!"[1]

9. ENTERTAINING A GROUP

✓ If you are given leeway and asked to speak to a group without any specific purpose other than to entertain, perhaps with the goal of "warming them up," carefully plan about four or five stories or activities—depending on desired length—and choose something funny or intriguing about each.

✓ Remember that being funny is great, but intriguing stories without humor are also entertaining. Anything with a mystery or an unexpected twist can work. For example, suppose you are asked to warm up an audience for a sports award banquet. You could do worse that a presentation on "The Five Most Athletic American Presidents" or "The Most Lopsided Losses in Baseball History."

✓ Use interactive activities. Homemade bingo games with answers to questions relevant to the main theme of the day or night can be surprisingly engaging. Polls and guessing games work well too.

✓ If you are expected to be funny but don't have confidence in your joke-telling ability, try for the type of humor outlined in Chapter 9—clearly topical (somehow related to the subject at hand), self-deprecating, and without an obvious punch line that will leave you hanging if the audience doesn't laugh.

✓ If you are expected to be funny and do have confidence that you can handle jokes, make a list but don't necessarily stick to the list. The key to this type of presentation is to be able to pull up a joke when appropriate. So over-plan, memorize, and go with the flow.

✓ Appear confident, even if you are not. Keep the presentation moving, even if the jokes are dying.

✓ Aim for about four laughs per minute, or more if you have a lot of one-liners.

✓ The standard close to an entertainment segment is to thank audiences for their attention, briefly and, oddly enough, with sincerity and dignity, even if the bit included a lot of screwball comedy. A line I've seen work well is something like, "Thanks so much. I really appreciate how nice you've been tonight. Treat every performer like you treated me, and you'll never see a bad show."

10. DELIVERING A KEYNOTE

✓ Gather a great deal of material, because you may be expected to speak for up to 45 minutes. While the precise definition of the term "keynote address" is not agreed upon universally, it generally means a speech that opens or closes an event and captures the overall essence of what the occasion is about.

✓ As the audience is filing in, circulate from table to table, especially the ones in distant territory. A large audience is unlike a smaller one, in that people at the sides and rear tend to tune out because of the distance and relative isolation. Seriously, in large halls, a person in the back may have trouble distinguishing your facial features. An in-person appearance before the talk provides the personal link that the actual presentation may not be able to supply.

✓ Open strong, usually with a great anecdote, and if possible a funny one.

✓ If you use slides, do so judiciously, and make sure they are impactful. Keynotes benefit from artistic, funny, or abstract slides, rather than informational bullet points. Some keynote speakers put Twitter tweets on slides for emphasis.

✓ You may want to include 10 or so main points. Be sure that within those points, there is some material that inspires, some that informs, some that motivates, and some that persuades. The keynote speech is usually is a blend of all the attributes of other presentations, which is why I presented this template last. Just be sure to go easy on the "sales" aspect; audiences generally want a show, not a sales pitch.

✓ Weave in personal stories. You have latitude for self-indulgence here. The keynote is the most show-biz type of presentation when it comes to standard speaking assignments, and therefore it's expected that some of your personality will come through. A little celebrity status is conferred on you as part of the job.

✓ Throughout the keynote, keep everything congruent. While a keynote is the easiest type of speech in which to wander off track, it is also the type most damaged by a lack of focus.

✓ End on a clear call to action—or, if more appropriate, an inspirational or motivational message. This is a show, and shows end with a climax.

Chapter 12

The Ten Techniques in Action: Classic Demonstrations and Explanations of the "Present Like a Pro" Techniques in Various Presentation Scenarios

This chapter offers some outstanding presentations, with my analysis and commentary presented in italics at the beginning and within the text.

My collection is eclectic and is not meant to be a listing of the greatest oratory in history, although the selections, by and large, are brilliant. I have chosen these works because they are good exemplars of different approaches, are accessible, and in many cases are memorable to the point of having become part of our vocabulary. For example, in this collection I have a speech given by former FCC chairman Newton Minow. You may not recognize the name, but you will certainly recognize the phrase "vast wasteland"—his reference to how he perceived the state of television at the time. I included it not only for that reason but also because it was such a good speech that it took a relatively obscure government official and an issue that no one particularly cared about and made both the man and the concept blink brightly on our radar for decades to come.

Some of the selections are classic, from what may be the most stirring call to action in history, Patrick Henry's call for liberty, to a magnificent

TED Talk (I'll explain that in a second) by a cooking and nutrition expert who absolutely dazzled an audience already accustomed to fine presentations.

You can find Jamie Oliver's TED Talk online, as well as many of the other selections here. Just do a quick Web search. I won't list the URLs, because it would take you more time to type them in than it would to watch the speeches. While there wasn't a camcorder in the audience for Patrick Henry's demand for freedom, there are some fine reenactments available.

Jamie Oliver's TED Talk: An Informative and Motivational Speech

I think this may have been the best TED Talk ever presented. In case you are not familiar with TED Talks—presentations that started by focusing on technology, entertainment, and design but evolved to cover just about any topic— visit TED.com, where you can see videos of these outstanding examples. TED Talks have turned into a premier international presentation showcase.

In this TED Talk, notice how skillfully humor is woven into the context, in much the same ways that were discussed in Chapter 9. Note, too, how Oliver introduces his main argument, states his case, outlines his main points, proves his case, counters conflicting arguments, concludes by showing how he has made the case, and closes with some self-deprecating humor—the structure outline in Chapter 1, Step 2. The pacing is flawless, and this transcript is annotated with times so that you can visualize the flow of his material.

Teach Every Child About Food

[00:11] Sadly, in the next 18 minutes when I do our chat, four Americans that are alive will be dead through the food that they eat.

[00:25] My name's Jamie Oliver. I'm 34 years old. I'm from Essex in England and for the last seven years I've worked fairly tirelessly to save lives in my own way. I'm not a doctor; I'm a chef, I don't have expensive equipment or medicine. I use information, education.

[00:50] I profoundly believe that the power of food has a primal place in our homes that binds us to the best bits of life. We have an awful, awful reality right now. America, you're at the top of your game. This is one of the most unhealthy countries in the world.

[01:16] Can I please just see a raise of hands for how many of you have children in this room today? Put your hands up. You can continue to put your hands up, aunties and uncles as well. Most of you. OK. We, the adults of the last four generations, have blessed our children with the destiny of a shorter lifespan than their own parents. Your child will live a life ten years younger than you because of the landscape of food that we've built around them. Two-thirds of this room, today, in America, are statistically overweight or obese. You lot, you're all right, but we'll get you eventually, don't worry.

[01:58] (Laughter)

Oliver has engaged the audience with humor, and now he uses his opening hook to move into the main thrust . . .

[01:59] The statistics of bad health are clear, very clear. We spend our lives being paranoid about death, murder, homicide, you name it; it's on the front page of every paper, CNN. Look at homicide at the bottom, for God's sake. Right?

[02:16] (Laughter)

[02:17] (Applause)

[02:22] Every single one of those in the red is a diet-related disease. Any doctor, any specialist will tell you that. Fact: diet-related disease is the biggest killer in the United States, right now, here today. This is a global problem. It's a catastrophe. It's sweeping the world. England is right behind you, as usual.

[02:47] (Laughter)

[02:51] I know they were close, but not that close. We need a revolution. Mexico, Australia, Germany, India, China, all have massive problems of obesity and bad health. Think about smoking. It costs way less than obesity now. Obesity costs you Americans 10 percent of your health-care bills, 150 billion dollars a year. In 10 years, it's set to double: 300 billion dollars a year. Let's be honest, guys, you haven't got that cash.

[03:23] (Laughter)

[03:27] I came here to start a food revolution that I so profoundly believe in. We need it. The time is now. We're in a tipping-point moment. I've been doing this for seven years. I've been trying in America for seven years. Now is the time when it's ripe—ripe for the picking. I went to the eye of the storm. I went to West Virginia, the most unhealthy state in America. Or it was last year. We've got a new one this year, but we'll work on that next season.

Again, more humor to keep the audience engaged.

[03:55] (Laughter)

[03:57] Huntington, West Virginia. Beautiful town. I wanted to put heart and soul and people, your public, around the statistics that we've become so used to. I want to introduce you to some of the people that I care about: your public, your children. I want to show a picture of my friend Brittany. She's 16 years old. She's got six years to live because of the food that she's eaten. She's the third generation of Americans that hasn't grown up within a food environment where they've been taught to cook at home or in school, or her mom, or her mom's mom. She has six years to live. She's eating her liver to death.

[04:39] Stacy, the Edwards family. This is a normal family, guys. Stacy does her best, but she's third-generation as well; she was never taught to cook at home or at school. The family's obese. Justin here, 12 years old, he's 350 pounds. He gets bullied, for God's sake. The daughter there, Katie, she's four years old. She's obese before she even gets to primary school. Marissa, she's all right, she's one of your lot. But you know what? Her father, who was obese, died in her arms, And then the second most important man in her life, her uncle, died of obesity, and now her step-dad is obese. You see, the thing is, obesity and diet-related disease doesn't just hurt the people that have it; it's all of their friends, families, brothers, sisters.

Stories keep the talk moving. Always think about stories and examples.

[05:26] Pastor Steve: an inspirational man, one of my early allies in Huntington, West Virginia. He's at the sharp knife-edge of this problem. He has to bury the people, OK? And he's fed up with it. He's fed up with burying his friends, his family, his community. Come winter, three times as many people die. He's sick of it. This is preventable disease. Waste of life. By the way, this is what they get buried in. We're not geared up to do this. Can't even get them out the door, and I'm being serious. Can't even get them there. Forklift.

[06:02] OK, I see it as a triangle, OK? This is our landscape of food. I need you to understand it. You've probably heard all this before. Over the last 30 years, what's happened that's ripped the heart out of this country? Let's be frank and honest. Well, modern-day life.

[06:18] Let's start with the Main Street. Fast food has taken over the whole country; we know that. The big brands are some of the most important powers, powerful powers, in this country.

[06:29] (Sighs)

[06:30] Supermarkets as well. Big companies. Big companies. Thirty years ago, most of the food was largely local and largely fresh. Now it's largely processed and full of all sorts of additives, extra ingredients, and you know the rest of the story. Portion size is obviously a massive, massive problem. Labeling is a massive problem. The labeling in this country is a disgrace. The industry wants to self-police themselves. What, in this kind of climate? They don't deserve it. How can you say something is low-fat when it's full of so much sugar?

Recall all the suggestions in this book about assembling a few main points and going through them one-by-one? Notice that's exactly what Oliver is doing. Tick ... tick ... tick. Always support the main takeaway, as explained in Chapter 1, Step 1.

[07:09] Home. The biggest problem with the home is that used to be the heart of passing on food culture, what made our society. That is not happening anymore. And you know, as we go to work and as life changes, and as life always evolves, we kind of have to look at it holistically—step back for a moment, and re-address the balance. It hasn't happened for 30 years, OK? I want to show you a situation that is very normal right now; the Edwards family.

[07:42] (Video) Jamie Oliver: Let's have a talk. This stuff goes through you and your family's body every week. And I need you to know that this is going to kill your children early. How are you feeling?

[07:57] Stacy: Just feeling really sad and depressed right now. But, you know, I want my kids to succeed in life and this isn't going to get them there. But I'm killing them.

[08:10] JO: Yes you are. You are. But we can stop that. Normal. Let's get on schools, something that I'm fairly much a specialist in. OK, school. What is school? Who invented it? What's the purpose of school? School was always invented to arm us with the tools to make us creative, do wonderful things, make us earn a living, etc., etc. You know, it's been kind of in this sort of tight box for a long, long time, OK? But we haven't really evolved it to deal with the health catastrophes of America, OK? School food is something that most kids—31 million a day, actually—have twice a day, more than often, breakfast and lunch, 180 days of the year. So you could say that school food is quite important, really, judging the circumstances.

[09:06] (Laughter)

[09:11] Before I crack into my rant, which I'm sure you're waiting for—

[09:15] (Laughter)

[09:19] I need to say one thing, and it's so important in, hopefully, the magic that happens and unfolds in the next three months. The lunch ladies, the lunch cooks of America—I offer myself as their ambassador. I'm not slagging them off. They're doing the best they can do. They're doing their best. But they're doing what they're told, and what they're being told to do is wrong. The system is highly run by accountants; there's not enough, or any, food-knowledgeable people in the business. There's a problem: If you're not a food expert, and you've got tight budgets and it's getting tighter, then you can't be creative, you can't duck and dive and write different things around things. If you're an accountant, and a box-ticker, the only thing you can do in these circumstances is buy cheaper shit.

[10:08] Now, the reality is, the food that your kids get every day is fast food, it's highly processed, there's not enough fresh food in there at all. You know, the amount of additives, E numbers, ingredients you wouldn't believe—there's not enough veggies at all. French fries are considered a vegetable. Pizza for breakfast. They don't even get crockery. Knives and forks? No, they're too dangerous. They have scissors in the classroom, but knives and forks? No. And the way I look at it is: If you don't have knives and forks in your school, you're purely endorsing, from a state level, fast food, because it's handheld. And yes, by the way, it is fast food: It's sloppy Joes, it's burgers, it's wieners, it's pizzas, it's all of that stuff.

[10:49] (Sighs)

[10:51] Ten percent of what we spend on health care, as I said earlier, is on obesity, and it's going to double. We're not teaching our kids. There's no statutory right to teach kids about food, elementary or secondary school, OK? We don't teach kids about food, right? And this is a little clip from an elementary school, which is very common in England.

[11:12] (Video) Who knows what this is?

Here's a good example of how interactivity with the audience rivets attention.

[11:14] Child: Potatoes.

[11:15] Jamie Oliver: Potato? So, you think these are potatoes? Do you know what that is? Do you know what that is?

[11:20] Child: Broccoli?

[11:22] JO: What about this? Our good old friend.

[11:24] Child: Celery.

[11:25] JO: No. What do you think this is?

[11:27] Child: Onion. JO: Onion? No.

[11:29] JO: Immediately you get a really clear sense of "Do the kids know anything about where food comes from?" Who knows what that is? Child: Uh, pear?

[11:36] JO: What do you think this is? Child: I don't know.

[11:39] JO: If the kids don't know what stuff is, then they will never eat it.

[11:44] (Laughter)

[11:46] JO: Normal. England and America, England and America. Guess what fixed that. Two one-hour sessions. We've got to start teaching our kids about food in schools, period.

[12:00] (Applause)

[12:05] I want to tell you about something that kind of epitomizes the trouble that we're in, guys, OK? I want to talk about something so basic as milk. Every kid has the right to milk at school. Your kids will be having milk at school, breakfast and lunch, right? They'll be having two bottles, OK? And most kids do. But milk ain't good enough anymore. Don't get me wrong, I support milk—but someone at the milk board probably paid a lot of money for some geezer to work out that if you put loads of flavorings, colorings and sugar in milk, more kids will drink it. Yeah.

[12:44] Obviously now that's going to catch on the apple board is going to work out that if they make toffee apples they'll eat more as well. Do you know what I mean? For me, there isn't any need to flavor the milk. Okay? There's sugar in everything. I know the ins and outs of those ingredients. It's in everything. Even the milk hasn't escaped the kind of modern-day problems. There's our milk. There's our carton. In that is nearly as much sugar as one of your favorite cans of fizzy pop, and they are having two a day. So, let me just show you. We've got one kid, here—having, you know, eight tablespoons of sugar a day. You know, there's your week. There's your month. And I've taken the liberty of putting in just the five years of elementary school sugar, just from milk. Now, I don't know about you guys, but judging the circumstances, right, any judge in the whole world would look at the statistics and the evidence, and they would find any government of old guilty of child abuse. That's my belief.

[13:56] (Applause)

[14:03] (Applause ends)

[14:04] Now, if I came up here, and I wish I could come up here today and hang a cure for AIDS or cancer, you'd be fighting and scrambling to get to me. This, all this bad news, is preventable. That's the good news. It's very, very preventable. So, let's just think about, we got a problem here, we need to reboot. Okay so, in my world, what do we need to do? Here is the thing, right, it cannot just come from one source. To reboot and make real tangible change, real change, so that I could look you in the white of the eyes and say, "In 10 years' time, the history of your children's lives, happiness—and let's not forget, you're clever if you eat well, you know you're going to live longer—all of that stuff, it will look different. OK?"

[14:52] So, supermarkets. Where else do you shop so religiously? Week in, week out. How much money do you spend, in your life, in a supermarket? Love them. They just sell us what we want. All right. They owe us to put a food ambassador in every major supermarket. They need to help us shop. They need to show us how to cook quick, tasty, seasonal meals for people that are busy. This is not expensive. It is done in some, and it needs to be done across the board in America soon, and quick. The big brands, you know, the food brands, need to put food education at the heart of their businesses. I know, easier said than done. It's the future. It's the only way.

[15:33] Fast food. With the fast-food industry you know, it's very competitive. I've had loads of secret papers and dealings with fast food restaurants. I know how they do it. I mean, basically they've weaned us on to these hits of sugar, salt and fat, and x, y, and z, and everyone loves them, right? So, these guys are going to be part of the solution. But we need to get the government to work with all of the fast food purveyors and the restaurant industry, and over a five, six, seven year period wean of us off the extreme amounts of fat, sugar and all the other non-food ingredients.

[16:08] Now, also, back to the sort of big brands: labeling, I said earlier, is an absolute farce and has got to be sorted. OK, school. Obviously, in schools, we owe it to them to make sure those 180 days of the year, from that little precious age of four, until 18, 20, 24, whatever, they need to be cooked proper, fresh food from local growers on site, OK? There needs to be a new standard of fresh, proper food for your children, yeah?

[16:38] (Applause)

[16:43] Under the circumstances, it's profoundly important that every single American child leaves school knowing how to cook 10 recipes that will save their life. Life skills.

[16:55] (Applause)

[16:57] That means that they can be students, young parents, and be able to sort of duck and dive around the basics of cooking, no matter what recession hits them next time. If you can cook, recession money doesn't matter. If you can cook, time doesn't matter. The workplace, we haven't really talked about it. You know, it's now time for corporate responsibility to really look at what they feed or make available to their staff. The staff are the moms and dads of America's children. Marissa, her father died in her hands, I think she'd be quite happy if corporate America could start feeding their staff properly. Definitely they shouldn't be left out. Let's go back to the home.

[17:37] Now, look, if we do all this stuff, and we can, it's so achievable. You can care and be commercial. Absolutely. But the home needs to start passing on cooking again, for sure. For sure, pass it on as a philosophy. And for me, it's quite romantic, but it's about if one person teaches three people how to cook something, and they teach three of their mates, that only has to repeat itself 25 times, and that's the whole population of America. Romantic, yes, but most importantly, it's about trying to get people to realize that every one of your individual efforts makes a difference. We've got to put back what's been lost. Huntington's Kitchen. Huntington, where I made this program, we've got this prime-time program that hopefully will inspire people to really get on this change. I truly believe that change will happen. Huntington's Kitchen. I work with a community. I worked in the schools. I found local sustainable funding to get every single school in the area from the junk, onto the fresh food: six-and-a-half grand per school.

[18:39] (Applause)

Okay, we've talked about the problem and are now talking about the solution. As I advised, a problem/solution structure is persuasive and easy to follow.

[18:41] That's all it takes, six-and-a-half grand per school. The Kitchen is 25 grand a month. Okay? This can do 5,000 people a year, which is 10 percent of their population, and it's people on people. You know, it's local cooks teaching local people. It's free cooking lessons, guys, in the Main Street. This is real, tangible change, real, tangible change. Around America, if we just look back now, there is plenty of wonderful things going on. There is plenty of beautiful things going on. There are angels around America doing great things in schools—farm-to-school set-ups, garden set-ups, education—there are amazing people doing this already. The problem is they all want to roll out what they're doing to the next school, but there's no cash. We need to recognize the experts and the angels quickly, identify them, and allow them to easily find the resource to keep rolling out what they're already doing, and doing well. Businesses of America need to support Mrs. Obama to do the things that she wants to do.

[19:44] (Applause)

[19:51] And look, I know it's weird having an English person standing here before you talking about all this. All I can say is: I care. I'm a father, and I love this country. And I believe truly, actually, that if change can be made in this country, beautiful things will happen around the world. If America does it, other people will follow. It's incredibly important.

Remember my advice on the versatility of self-deprecating humor? See how it works at the end.

[20:14] (Audience) Yeah!

[20:15] (Applause)

[20:21] When I was in Huntington, trying to get a few things to work when they weren't, I thought "If I had a magic wand, what would I do?" And I thought, "You know what? I'd just love to be put in front of some of the most amazing movers and shakers in America." And a month later, TED phoned me up and gave me this award. I'm here. So, my wish. Dyslexic, so I'm a bit slow. My wish is for you to help a strong, sustainable movement to educate every child about food, to inspire families to cook again, and to empower people everywhere to fight obesity.

[21:20] (Applause)
[21:31] Thank you.
[21:32] (Applause continues)

Source: JAMIE OLIVER, TED 2010. Reprinted with Permission of TED Media Requests.

A COMMEMORATIVE SPEECH

Ronald Reagan

Address to the Nation on the Explosion of the Space Shuttle *Challenger*

January 28, 1986

As I said, this is not a collection of the world's greatest oratory, but when people do make such lists, this speech is usually somewhere near the top.

Shortly after the space shuttle Challenger *exploded, killing six crew members and a civilian teacher, Reagan canceled his planned State of the Union address, and speechwriter Peggy Noonan was asked to craft words that would somehow reassure the audience that Americans would endure and that life would go on. Note how there is movement within this piece—the idea that we will endure an ordeal and emerge as a victor—the type of "mythic" structure discussed in Chapter 1, Step 2.*

Ladies and gentlemen, I'd planned to speak to you tonight to report on the state of the Union, but the events of earlier today have led me to change those plans. Today is a day for mourning and remembering. Nancy and I are pained to the core by the tragedy of the shuttle *Challenger*. We know we share this pain with all of the people of our country. This is truly a national loss.

Nineteen years ago, almost to the day, we lost three astronauts in a terrible accident on the ground. But we've never lost an astronaut in flight; we've never had a tragedy like this. And perhaps we've forgotten the courage it took for the crew of the shuttle. But they, the *Challenger* Seven, were aware of the dangers, but overcame them and did their jobs brilliantly. We mourn seven heroes: Michael Smith, Dick Scobee, Judith Resnik, Ronald McNair, Ellison Onizuka, Gregory Jarvis, and Christa McAuliffe. We mourn their loss as a nation together.

Here we have the proper formality in commemorating the loss of life—a slow and dignified reading of the names.

For the families of the seven, we cannot bear, as you do, the full impact of this tragedy. But we feel the loss, and we're thinking about you so very much. Your loved ones were daring and brave, and they had that special grace, that special spirit that says, "Give me a challenge, and I'll meet it with joy." They had a hunger to explore the universe and discover its truths. They wished to serve, and they did. They served all of us. We've grown used to wonders in this century. It's hard to dazzle us. But for 25 years the United States space program has been doing just that. We've grown used to the idea of space, and perhaps we forget that we've only just begun. We're still pioneers. They, the members of the *Challenger* crew, were pioneers.

And I want to say something to the schoolchildren of America who were watching the live coverage of the shuttle's takeoff. I know it is hard to understand, but sometimes painful things like this happen. It's all part of the process of exploration and discovery. It's all part of taking a chance and expanding man's horizons. The future doesn't belong to the fainthearted; it belongs to the brave. The *Challenger* crew was pulling us into the future, and we'll continue to follow them.

Above is probably the most famous line of the presentation and one of the most famous lines in all of modern oratory. It's an example of making one point clearly and making the entire presentation stick to that point.

I've always had great faith in and respect for our space program, and what happened today does nothing to diminish it. We don't hide our space program. We don't keep secrets and cover things up. We do it all up front and in public. That's the way freedom is, and we wouldn't change it for a minute. We'll continue our quest in space. There will be more shuttle flights and more shuttle crews and, yes, more volunteers, more civilians, more teachers in space. Nothing ends here; our hopes and our journeys continue. I want to add that I wish I could talk to every man and woman who works for NASA or who worked on this mission and tell them: "Your dedication and professionalism have moved and impressed us for decades. And we know of your anguish. We share it."

There's a coincidence today. On this day 390 years ago, the great explorer Sir Francis Drake died aboard ship off the coast of Panama. In his lifetime the great frontiers were the oceans, and an historian later said, "He lived by the sea, died on it, and was buried in it." Well, today we can say of the *Challenger* crew: Their dedication was, like Drake's, complete.

And we've just had an emotional quote that begins the ending and in the process ties everything together.

The crew of the space shuttle *Challenger* honored us by the manner in which they lived their lives. We will never forget them, nor the last time we saw them, this morning, as they prepared for their journey and waved goodbye and "slipped the surly bonds of earth" to "touch the face of God."

BUSINESS AND POLICY PRESENTATION TO A FAIRLY UNSYMPATHETIC AUDIENCE

Newton N. Minow

Television and the Public Interest

May 9, 1961, National Association of Broadcasters, Washington, D.C.

This is one of the most influential speeches in history related to the mass media, and more than 50 years after its debut, we still use its framework and vocabulary to debate the state of media. It was delivered before the National Association of Broadcasters convention in 1961. This was not an entirely friendly audience, as Minow was being quite critical of the industry.

Notice how Minow skillfully presents a problem and then offers a solution (Chapter 2, Step 8). Note, too, how he uses a lot of statistics but manages to frame them coherently in his narrative (Chapter 3, Step 9).

Governor Collins, distinguished guests, ladies and gentlemen. Governor Collins, you're much too kind, as all of you have been to me the last few days. It's been a great pleasure and an honor for me to meet so many of you. And I want to thank you for this opportunity to meet with you today.

As you know, this is my first public address since I took over my new job. When the New Frontiersmen rode into town, I locked myself in my office to do my homework and get my feet wet. But apparently I haven't managed yet to stay out of hot water. I seem to have detected a very nervous apprehension about what I might say or do when I emerged from that locked office for this, my maiden station break.

So first let me begin by dispelling a rumor. I was not picked for this job because I regard myself as the fastest draw on the New Frontier. Second, let me start a rumor. Like you, I have carefully read President Kennedy's messages about the regulatory agencies, conflict of interest, and the dangers of ex parte contacts. And, of course, we at the Federal Communications Commission will do our part. Indeed, I may even suggest that we change the name of the FCC to The Seven Untouchables.

The opening breaks the ice, and the ice might have been pretty thick and frosty …

It may also come as a surprise to some of you, but I want you to know that you have my admiration and my respect. Yours is a most honorable profession. Anyone who is in the broadcasting business has a tough row to hoe. You earn your bread by using public property. When you work in broadcasting you volunteer for public service, public pressure, and public regulation. You must compete with other attractions and other investments, and the only way you can do it is to prove to us every three years that you should have been in business in the first place.

I can think of easier ways to make a living.

But I cannot think of more satisfying ways.

I admire your courage—but that doesn't mean that I would make life any easier for you. Your license lets you use the public's airwaves as trustees for 180 million Americans. The public is your beneficiary. If you want to stay on as trustees, you must deliver a decent return to the public—not only to your stockholders. So, as a representative of the public, your health and your product are among my chief concerns.

Now as to your health, let's talk only of television today. 1960 gross broadcast revenues of the television industry were over 1,268,000,000 dollars. Profit before taxes was 243,900,000 dollars, an average return on revenue of 19.2 per cent. Compare these with 1959, when gross broadcast revenues were 1,163,900,000 dollars, and profit before taxes was 222,300,000, an average return on revenue of 19.1 per cent. So the percentage increase of total revenues from '59 to '60 was 9 per cent, and the percentage increase of profit was 9.7 per cent. This, despite a recession throughout the country. For your investors, the price has indeed been right.

So I have confidence in your health, but not in your product. It is with this and much more in mind that I come before you today.

One editorialist in the trade press wrote that "the FCC of the New Frontier is going to be one of the toughest FCCs in the history of broadcast regulation." If he meant that we intend to enforce the law in the public interest, let me make it perfectly clear that he is right: We do. If he meant that we intend to muzzle or censor broadcasting, he is dead wrong. It wouldn't surprise me if some of you had expected me to come here today and say to you in effect, "Clean up your own house or the government will do it for you." Well, in a limited sense, you would be right because I've just said it.

But I want to say to you as earnestly as I can that it is not in that spirit that I come before you today, nor is it in that spirit that I intend to serve the FCC. I am in Washington to help broadcasting, not to harm it; to strengthen it, not weaken it; to reward it, not to punish it; to encourage it, not threaten it; and to stimulate it, not censor it. Above all, I am here to uphold and protect the public interest.

Now what do we mean by "the public interest"? Some say the public interest is merely what interests the public. I disagree. And so does your distinguished president, Governor Collins. In a recent speech—and of course as I also told you yesterday—In a recent speech he said,

Notice the rhythmic phrasing: a drumbeat of contentions ...

Broadcasting to serve the public interest, must have a soul and a conscience, a burning desire to excel, as well as to sell; the urge to build the character, citizenship, and intellectual stature of people, as well as to expand the gross national product.... By no means do I imply that broadcasters disregard the public interest.... But a much better job can be done, and should be done.

I could not agree more with Governor Collins. And I would add that in today's world, with chaos in Laos and the Congo aflame, with Communist tyranny on our Caribbean doorstep, relentless pressures on our Atlantic alliance, with social and economic problems at home of the gravest nature, yes, and with the technological knowledge that makes it possible, as our President has said, not only to destroy our world but to destroy poverty around the world—in a time of peril and opportunity, the old complacent, unbalanced fare of action-adventure and situation comedies is simply not good enough.

Your industry possesses the most powerful voice in America. It has an inescapable duty to make that voice ring with intelligence and with leadership. In a few years, this exciting industry has grown from a novelty to an instrument of overwhelming impact on the American people. It should be making ready for the kind of leadership that newspapers and magazines assumed years ago, to make our people aware of their world.

Ours has been called the jet age, the atomic age, the space age. It is also, I submit, the television age. And just as history will decide whether the leaders of today's world employed the atom to destroy the world or rebuild it for mankind's benefit, so will history decide whether today's broadcasters employed their powerful voice to enrich the people or to debase them.

Above is a very emotional (pathos) *appeal.*

If I seem today to address myself chiefly to the problems of television, I don't want any of you radio broadcasters to think that we've gone to sleep at your switch. We haven't. We still listen. But in recent years most of the controversies and cross-currents in broadcast programming have swirled around television. And so my subject today is the television industry and the public interest.

Like everybody, I wear more than one hat. I am the chairman of the FCC. But I am also a television viewer and the husband and father of other television viewers. I have seen a great many television programs that seemed to me eminently worthwhile and I am not talking about the much bemoaned good old days of "Playhouse 90" and "Studio One."

I'm talking about this past season. Some were wonderfully entertaining, such as "The Fabulous Fifties," "The Fred Astaire Show," and "The Bing Crosby Special"; some were dramatic and moving, such as Conrad's "Victory" and "Twilight Zone"; some were marvelously informative, such as "The Nation's Future," "CBS Reports," "The Valiant Years." I could list many more—programs that I am sure everyone here felt enriched his own life and that of his family. When television is good, nothing—not the theater, not the magazines or newspapers—nothing is better.

And coming is the famous line ...

But when television is bad, nothing is worse. I invite each of you to sit down in front of your television set when your station goes on the air and stay there, for a day, without a book, without a magazine, without a newspaper, without a profit and loss sheet or a rating book to distract you. Keep your eyes glued to that set until the station signs off. I can assure you that what you will observe is a vast wasteland.

Stories, stories, stories! As advised in Chapter 2, Step 2, don't just dump data ... tell stories.

You will see a procession of game shows, formula comedies about totally unbelievable families, blood and thunder, mayhem, violence, sadism, murder, western bad men, western good men, private eyes, gangsters, more violence, and cartoons. And endlessly, commercials—many screaming, cajoling, and offending. And most of all, boredom. True, you'll see a few things you will enjoy. But they will be very, very few. And if you think I exaggerate, I only ask you to try it.

Is there one person in this room who claims that broadcasting can't do better? Well, a glance at next season's proposed programming can give us little heart. Of 73 and 1/2 hours of prime evening time, the networks have tentatively scheduled 59 hours of categories of action-adventure, situation comedy, variety, quiz, and movies. Is there one network president in this room who claims he can't do better? Well, is there at least one network president who believes that the other networks can do better? Gentlemen, your trust accounting with your beneficiaries is long overdue. Never have so few owed so much to so many.

Why is so much of television so bad? I've heard many answers: demands of your advertisers; competition for ever higher ratings; the need always to attract a mass audience; the high cost of television programs; the insatiable appetite for programming material. These are some of the reasons. Unquestionably, these are tough problems not susceptible to easy answers. But I am not convinced that you have tried hard enough to solve them.

I do not accept the idea that the present over-all programming is aimed accurately at the public taste. The ratings tell us only that some people have their television sets turned on and of that number, so many are tuned to one channel and so many to another. They don't tell us what the public might watch if they were offered half-a-dozen additional choices. A rating, at best, is an indication of how many people saw what you gave them. Unfortunately, it does not reveal the depth of the penetration, or the intensity of reaction, and it never reveals what the acceptance would have been if what you gave them had been better—if all the forces of art and creativity and daring and imagination had been unleashed. I believe in the people's good sense and good taste, and I am not convinced that the people's taste is as low as some of you assume.

Here's a good spot to revive audience attention with a question. What can we do? Tension and release (Chapter 2, Step 4).

My concern with the rating services is not with their accuracy. Perhaps they are accurate. I really don't know. What, then, is wrong with the ratings? It's not been their accuracy—it's been their use.

Certainly, I hope you will agree that ratings should have little influence where children are concerned. The best estimates indicate that during the hours of 5 to 6 P.M. sixty per cent of your audience is composed of children under twelve. And most young children today, believe it or not, spend as much time watching television as they do in the schoolroom. I repeat—let that sink in, ladies and gentlemen—most young children today spend as much time watching television as they do in the schoolroom. It used to be said that there were three great influences on a child: home, school, and church. Today, there is a fourth great influence, and you ladies and gentlemen in this room control it.

If parents, teachers, and ministers conducted their responsibilities by following the ratings, children would have a steady diet of ice cream, school holidays, and no Sunday school. What about your responsibilities? Is there no room on television to teach, to inform, to uplift, to stretch, to enlarge the capacities of our children? Is there no room for programs deepening their understanding of children in other lands? Is there no room for a children's news show explaining something to them about the world at their level of understanding? Is there no room for reading the great literature of the past, for teaching them the great traditions of freedom? There are some fine children's shows, but they are drowned out in the massive doses of cartoons, violence, and more violence. Must these be your trademarks? Search your consciences and see if you cannot offer more to your young beneficiaries whose future you guide so many hours each and every day.

Another question and answer. A great technique ...

Now what about adult programming and ratings? You know, newspaper publishers take popularity ratings too. And the answers are pretty clear: It is almost always the comics, followed by advice to the lovelorn columns. But, ladies and gentlemen, the news is still on the front page of all newspapers; the editorials are not replaced by more comics; and the newspapers have not become one long collection of advice to the lovelorn. Yet newspapers do not even need a license from the government to be in business; they do not use public property. But in television, where your responsibilities as public trustees are so plain, the moment that the ratings indicate that westerns are popular there are new imitations of westerns on the air faster than the old coaxial cable could take us from Hollywood to New York. Broadcasting cannot continue to live by the numbers. Ratings ought to be the slave of the broadcaster, not his master. And you and I both know—You and I both know that the rating services themselves would agree.

Let me make clear that what I am talking about is balance. I believe that the public interest is made up of many interests. There are many people in this great country and you must serve all of us. You will get no argument from me if you say that, given a choice between a western and a symphony, more people will watch the western. I like westerns too, but a steady diet for the whole country is obviously not in the public interest. We all know that people would more often prefer to be entertained than stimulated or informed. But your obligations are not satisfied if you look only to popularity as a test of what to broadcast. You are not only in show business; you are free to communicate ideas as well as relaxation.

And as Governor Collins said to you yesterday when he encouraged you to editorialize—as you know the FCC has now encouraged editorializing for years. We want you to do this; we want you to editorialize, take positions. We only ask that you do it in a fair and a responsible manner. Those stations that have editorialized have demonstrated to you that the FCC will always encourage a fair and responsible clash of opinion.

Now, proposed solutions ...

You must provide a wider range of choices, more diversity, more alternatives. It is not enough to cater to the nation's whims; you must also serve the nation's needs. And I would add this: that if some of you persist in a relentless search for the highest rating and the lowest common denominator, you may very well lose your audience. Because, to paraphrase a great American who was recently my law partner, the people are wise, wiser than some of the broadcasters—and politicians—think.

As you may have gathered, I would like to see television improved. But how is this to be brought about? By voluntary action by the broadcasters themselves? By direct government intervention? Or how?

Let me address myself now to my role not as a viewer but as chairman of the FCC. I could not if I would, chart for you this afternoon in detail all of the actions I contemplate. Instead, I want to make clear some of the fundamental principles which guide me.

A very effective way to keep your talk organized: points number 1, 2, 3, 4, 5, and 6 (Chapter 1, Step 2.) . . .

First: the people own the air. And they own it as much in prime evening time as they do at six o'clock Sunday morning. For every hour that the people give you—you owe them something. And I intend to see that your debt is paid with service.

Second: I think it would be foolish and wasteful for us to continue any worn-out wrangle over the problems of payola, rigged quiz shows, and other mistakes of the past. There are laws on the books which we will enforce. But there is no chip on my shoulder. We live together in perilous, uncertain times; we face together staggering problems; and we must not waste much time now by rehashing the clichés of past controversy. To quarrel over the past is to lose the future.

Third: I believe in the free enterprise system. I want to—I want to see broadcasting improved, and I want you to do the job. I am proud to champion your cause. It is not rare for American businessmen to serve a public trust. Yours is a special trust because it is imposed by law.

Fourth: I will do all I can to help educational television. There are still not enough educational stations, and major centers of the country still lack usable educational channels. If there were a limited number of printing presses in this country, you may be sure that a fair proportion of them would be put to educational use. Educational television has an enormous contribution to make to the future, and I intend to give it a hand along the way. If there is not a nation-wide educational television system in this country, it will not be the fault of the FCC.

Fifth: I am unalterably opposed to governmental censorship. There will be no suppression of programming which does not meet with bureaucratic tastes. Censorship strikes at the taproot of our free society.

Sixth: I did not come to Washington to idly observe the squandering of the public's airwaves. The squandering of our airwaves is no less important than the lavish waste of any precious natural resource. I intend to take the job of chairman of the FCC very seriously. I happen to believe in the gravity of my own particular sector of the New Frontier. There will be times perhaps when you will consider that I take myself or my job too seriously. Frankly, I don't care if you do. For I am convinced that either one takes this job seriously—or one can be seriously taken.

Now how will these principles be applied? Clearly at the heart of the FCC's authority lies its power to license, to renew or fail to renew, or to revoke a license. As you know, when your license comes up for renewal, your performance is compared with your promises. I understand that many people feel that in the past licenses were often renewed pro forma. I say to you now: renewal will not be pro forma in the future. There is nothing permanent or sacred about a broadcast license.

But simply matching promises and performance is not enough. I intend to do more. I intend to find out whether the people care. I intend to find out whether the community which each broadcaster serves believes he has been serving the public interest. When a renewal is set down for a hearing, I intend, whenever possible, to hold a well-advertised public hearing, right in the community you have promised to serve. I want the people who own the air and the homes that television enters to tell you and the FCC what's been going on. I want the people—if they're truly interested in the service you give them—to make notes, document cases, tell us the facts. And for those few of you who really believe that the public interest is merely what interests the public, I hope that these hearings will arouse no little interest.

The FCC has a fine reserve of monitors—almost 180 million Americans gathered around 56 million sets. If you want those monitors to be your friends at court, it's up to you.

Counter objections. Remember the structure outline in Chapter 2, Step 1—state your case, outline your main points, prove your case, counter conflicting arguments, and conclude by showing how you have made your case? Here's how you do it:

Now some of you may say, "Yes, but I still do not know where the line is between a grant of a renewal and the hearing you just spoke of." My answer is: Why should you want to know how close you can come to the edge of the cliff? What the Commission asks of you is to make a conscientious, good-faith effort to serve the public interest. Every one of you serves a community in which the people would benefit by educational, and religious, instructive and other public service programming. Every one of you serves an area which has local needs—as to local elections, controversial issues, local news, local talent. Make a serious, genuine effort to put on that programming. And when you do, you will not be playing brinkmanship with the public interest.

Now what I've been saying applies to the broadcast stations. Now a station break for the networks—which will last even longer than 40 seconds: You networks know your importance in this great industry. Today, more than one-half of all hours of television station programming comes from the networks; in prime time, this rises to more than three-fourths of the available hours.

You know that the FCC has been studying network operations for some time. I intend to press this to a speedy conclusion with useful results. I can tell you right now, however, that I am deeply concerned with concentration of power in the hands of the networks. As a result, too many local stations have foregone any efforts at local programming, with little use of live talent and local service. Too many local stations operate with one hand on the network switch and the other on a projector loaded with old movies. We want the individual stations to be free to meet their legal responsibilities to serve their communities.

I join Governor Collins in his views so well expressed to the advertisers who use the public air. And I urge the networks to join him and undertake a very special mission on behalf of this industry. You can tell your advertisers, "This is the high quality we are going to serve—take it or other people will. If you think you can find a better place to move automobiles, cigarettes, and soap, then go ahead and try." Tell your sponsors to be less concerned with costs per thousand and more concerned with understanding per millions. And remind your stockholders that an investment in broadcasting is buying a share in public responsibility. The networks can start this industry on the road to freedom from the dictatorship of numbers.

But there is more to the problem than network influences on stations or advertiser influences on networks. I know the problems networks face in trying to clear some of their best programs—the informational programs that exemplify public service. They are your finest hours, whether sustaining or commercial, whether regularly scheduled or special. These are the signs that broadcasting knows the way to leadership. They make the public's trust in you a wise choice.

They should be seen. As you know, we are readying for use new forms by which broadcast stations will report their programming to the Commission.

You probably also know that special attention will be paid in these forms to reports of public service programming. I believe that stations taking network service should also be required to report the extent of the local clearance of network public service programs, and when they fail to clear them, they should explain why. If it is to put on some outstanding local program, this is one reason. But if it is simply to run an old movie, that's an entirely different matter. And the Commission should consider such clearance reports carefully when making up its mind about the licensee's over-all programming.

We intend to move—and as you know, and as I want to say publicly, the FCC was rapidly moving in other new areas before the new Administration arrived in Washington. And I want to pay my public respects to my very able predecessor, Fred Ford, and to my colleagues on the Commission, each of whom has welcomed me to the FCC with warmth and cooperation.

We have approved an experiment with pay TV, and in New York we are testing the potential of UHF broadcasting. Either or both of these may revolutionize television. Only a foolish prophet would venture to guess the direction they will take, and their effect. But we intend that they shall be explored fully, for they are part of broadcasting's New Frontier. The questions surrounding pay TV are largely economic. The questions surrounding UHF are largely technological. We are going to give the infant—the infant pay TV a chance to prove whether it can offer a useful service; we are going to protect it from those who would strangle it in its crib.

As for UHF, I'm sure you know about our test in the canyons of New York City. We will take every possible positive step to break through the allocations barrier into UHF. We will put this sleeping giant to use and in the years ahead we may have twice as many channels operating in cities where now there are only two or three. We may have a half-dozen networks instead of three.

I have told you that I believe in the free enterprise system. I believe that most of television's problems stem from lack of competition. This is the importance of UHF to me: with more channels on the air, we will be able to provide every community with enough stations to offer service to all parts of the public. Programs with a mass market appeal required by mass product advertisers certainly will still be available. But other stations will recognize the need to appeal to more limited markets and to special tastes. In this way, we can all have a much wider range of programs. Television should thrive on this competition, and the country should benefit from alternative sources of service to the public. And, Governor Collins, I hope the NAB will benefit from many new members.

Another and perhaps the most important frontier: Television will rapidly join the parade into space. International television will be with us soon. No one knows how long it will be until a broadcast from a studio in New York will be viewed in India as well as in Indiana, will be seen in the Congo as it is seen in Chicago. But as surely as we are meeting here today, that day will come; and once again our world will shrink.

Attention revived again with a question …

What will the people of other countries think of us when they see our western bad men and good men punching each other in the jaw in between the shooting? What will the Latin American or African child learn of America from this great communications industry? We cannot permit television in its present form to be our voice overseas.

There is your challenge to leadership. You must reexamine some fundamentals of your industry. You must open your minds and open your hearts to the limitless horizons of tomorrow. I can suggest some words that should serve to guide you:

Television and all who participate in it are jointly accountable to the American public for respect for the special needs of children, for community responsibility, for the advancement of education and culture, for the acceptability of the program materials chosen, for decency and decorum in production, and for propriety in advertising. This responsibility cannot be discharged by any given group of programs, but can be discharged only through the highest standards of respect for the American home, applied to every moment of every program presented by television.

Program materials should enlarge the horizons of the viewer, provide him with wholesome entertainment, afford helpful stimulation, and remind him of the responsibilities which the citizen has towards his society.

Now those are not my words. They are yours. They are taken literally, verbatim, from your own Television Code. They reflect the leadership and aspirations of your own great industry. I urge you to respect them as I do. And I urge you to respect the intelligent and farsighted leadership of Governor LeRoy Collins, and to make this meeting a creative act. I urge you at this meeting and, after you leave, back home, at your stations and your networks, to strive ceaselessly to improve your product and to better serve your viewers, the American people.

I hope that we at the FCC will not allow ourselves to become so bogged down in the mountain of papers, hearings, memoranda, orders, and the daily routine that we close our eyes to this wider view of the public interest. And I hope that you broadcasters will not permit yourselves to become so absorbed in the daily chase for ratings, sales, and profits that you lose this wider view. Now more than ever before in broadcasting's history the times demand the best of all of us.

We need imagination in programming, not sterility; creativity, not imitation; experimentation, not conformity; excellence, not mediocrity. Television is filled with creative, imaginative people. You must strive to set them free.

Television in its young life has had many hours of greatness—its "Victory at Sea," its Army-McCarthy hearings, its "Peter Pan," its "Kraft Theaters," its "See It Now," its "Project 20," the World Series, its political conventions and campaigns, and the Great Debates. And it's had its endless hours of mediocrity and its moments of public disgrace. There are estimates today that the average viewer spends about 200 minutes daily with television, while the average reader spends 38 minutes with magazines, 40 minutes with newspapers. Television has grown faster than a teenager, and now it is time to grow up.

What you gentlemen broadcast through the people's air affects the people's taste, their knowledge, their opinions, their understanding of themselves and of their world—and their future.

Just think for a moment of the impact of broadcasting in the past few days. Yesterday was one of the great days of my life. Last week the President asked me to ride over with him when he came to speak here at the NAB. And when I went to the White House he said, "Do you think it would be a good idea to take Commander Shepard?" And, of course, I said it would be magnificent. And I was privileged to ride here yesterday in a car with the President and the Vice President, Commander and Mrs. Shepard. This was an unexpected, unscheduled stop. And Commander Shepard said to me, "Where are we going? What is this group?" And I said, "This is the National Association of Broadcasters at its annual convention."

This is the group, this is the industry that made it possible for millions of Americans to share with you that great moment in history; that his gallant flight was witnessed by millions of anxious Americans who saw in it an intimacy which they could achieve through no other medium, in no other way. It was one of your finest hours. The depth of broadcasting's contribution to public understanding of that event cannot be measured. And it thrilled me—as a representative of the government that deals with this industry—to say to Commander Shepard the group that he was about to see.

I say to you ladies and gentlemen—I remind you what the President said in his stirring inaugural. He said: Ask not what America can do for you; ask what you can do for America. I say to you ladies and gentlemen: Ask not what broadcasting can do for you; ask what you can do for broadcasting. And ask what broadcasting can do for America.

I urge you, I urge you to put the people's airwaves to the service of the people and the cause of freedom. You must help prepare a generation for great decisions. You must help a great nation fulfill its future.

Do this! I pledge you our help.

Thank you.
Source: www.americanrhetoric.com (public domain)[1]

A MOTIVATIONAL PRESENTATION WITH THE MOST FAMOUS CALL TO ACTION IN ALL OF SPEECH-MAKING HISTORY

Give Me Liberty Or Give Me Death

Patrick Henry, March 23, 1775

This is an excellent persuasive speech, and it is well-organized and compact. Notice how it flows from the introduction (the statement of what the speech is about), counters contrary arguments, and ends with a call to action. Cicero (Chapter 1, Step 2) would be proud.

The speech, with which we are almost all familiar, is actually a reconstruction. Most addresses weren't written down in that dangerous era in American history, but in the early 1800s, a Henry biographer pieced it together from what records and recollections existed.

Note how, as described in Chapter 2, Step 5, this address uses Aristotle's identified three "rhetorical appeals" called ethos, pathos, *and* logos. *Listeners were certainly persuaded by authority and qualification (ethos), appeals to emotion (pathos), and demonstrations of logic (logos). You won't have any trouble spotting those appeals in this masterpiece.*

No man thinks more highly than I do of the patriotism, as well as abilities, of the very worthy gentlemen who have just addressed the House. But different men often see the same subject in different lights; and, therefore, I hope it will not be thought disrespectful to those gentlemen if, entertaining as I do opinions of a character very opposite to theirs, I shall speak forth my sentiments freely and without reserve. This is no time for ceremony. The question before the House is one of awful moment to this country. For my own part, I consider it as nothing less than a question of freedom or slavery; and in proportion to the magnitude of the subject ought to be the freedom of the debate. It is only in this way that we can hope to arrive at truth, and fulfill the great responsibility which we hold to God and our country. Should I keep back my opinions at such a time, through fear of giving offense, I should consider myself as guilty of treason towards my country, and of an act of disloyalty toward the Majesty of Heaven, which I revere above all earthly kings.

Mr. President, it is natural to man to indulge in the illusions of hope. We are apt to shut our eyes against a painful truth, and listen to the song of that siren till she transforms us into beasts. Is this the part of wise men, engaged in a great and arduous struggle for liberty? Are we disposed to be of the number of those who, having eyes, see not, and, having ears, hear not, the things which so nearly concern their temporal salvation? For my part, whatever anguish of spirit it may cost, I am willing to know the whole truth; to know the worst, and to provide for it.

Now we get analogies and stories to make the presentation relatable.

I have but one lamp by which my feet are guided, and that is the lamp of experience. I know of no way of judging of the future but by the past. And judging by the past, I wish to know what there has been in the conduct of the British ministry for the last ten years to justify those hopes with which gentlemen have been pleased to solace themselves and the House. Is it that insidious smile with which our petition has been lately received? Trust it not, sir; it will prove a snare to your feet. Suffer not yourselves to be betrayed with a kiss.

Ask yourselves how this gracious reception of our petition comports with those warlike preparations which cover our waters and darken our land. Are fleets and armies necessary to a work of love and reconciliation? Have we shown ourselves so unwilling to be reconciled that force must be called in to win back our love? Let us not deceive ourselves, sir. These are the implements of war and subjugation; the last arguments to which kings resort.

Now a question brings the audience to attention . . .

I ask gentlemen, sir, what means this martial array, if its purpose be not to force us to submission? Can gentlemen assign any other possible motive for it? Has Great Britain any enemy, in this quarter of the world, to call for all this accumulation of navies and armies? No, sir, she has none. They are meant for us: they can be meant for no other. They are sent over to bind and rivet upon us those chains which the British ministry have been so long forging.

And what have we to oppose to them? Shall we try argument? Sir, we have been trying that for the last ten years. Have we anything new to offer upon the subject? Nothing. We have held the subject up in every light of which it is capable; but it has been all in vain. Shall we resort to entreaty and humble supplication? What terms shall we find which have not been already exhausted? Let us not, I beseech you, sir, deceive ourselves longer.

Now Henry answers the question . . .

Sir, we have done everything that could be done to avert the storm which is now coming on. We have petitioned; we have remonstrated; we have supplicated; we have prostrated ourselves before the throne, and have implored its interposition to arrest the tyrannical hands of the ministry and Parliament. Our petitions have been slighted; our remonstrances have produced additional violence and insult; our supplications have been disregarded; and we have been spurned, with contempt, from the foot of the throne!

In vain, after these things, may we indulge the fond hope of peace and reconciliation. There is no longer any room for hope. If we wish to be free— if we mean to preserve inviolate those inestimable privileges for which we have been so long contending—if we mean not basely to abandon the noble struggle in which we have been so long engaged, and which we have pledged ourselves never to abandon until the glorious object of our contest shall be obtained—we must fight! I repeat it, sir, we must fight! An appeal to arms and to the God of hosts is all that is left us!

They tell us, sir, that we are weak; unable to cope with so formidable an adversary. But when shall we be stronger? Will it be the next week, or the next year? Will it be when we are totally disarmed, and when a British guard shall be stationed in every house? Shall we gather strength by irresolution and inaction? Shall we acquire the means of effectual resistance by lying supinely on our backs and hugging the delusive phantom of hope, until our enemies shall have bound us hand and foot?

Sir, we are not weak if we make a proper use of those means which the God of nature hath placed in our power. Three millions of people, armed in the holy cause of liberty, and in such a country as that which we possess, are invincible by any force which our enemy can send against us.

Now comes the call to action. Remember the advice in Chapter 2, Step 7 to build your presentation around memorable phrases? Coming are several…

Besides, sir, we shall not fight our battles alone. There is a just God who presides over the destinies of nations, and who will raise up friends to fight our battles for us. The battle, sir, is not to the strong alone; it is to the vigilant, the active, the brave. Besides, sir, we have no election. If we were base enough to desire it, it is now too late to retire from the contest. There is no retreat but in submission and slavery! Our chains are forged! Their clanking may be heard on the plains of Boston! The war is inevitable—and let it come! I repeat it, sir, let it come.

It is in vain, sir, to extenuate the matter. Gentlemen may cry, peace, peace—but there is no peace. The war is actually begun! The next gale that sweeps from the north will bring to our ears the clash of resounding arms!

Our brethren are already in the field! Why stand we here idle? What is it that gentlemen wish? What would they have? Is life so dear, or peace so sweet, as to be purchased at the price of chains and slavery?

And now, the mother of all memorable phrases...

Forbid it, Almighty God! I know not what course others may take; but as for me, give me liberty or give me death![2]

PRESENTING AN AWARD

Carl Hausman

Wenonah, New Jersey, Hometown Legend Award, July 4, 2016

I know this isn't an earth-shattering address, but it does illustrate a couple of important points. As I mentioned in the template for presenting an award, you need to have two logistical issues under control: (1) name the person but don't have him or her come up yet, and (2) provide a moment where both you and the recipient are standing together as the award is presented.

Great job, volunteers who put all this together.

There are countless volunteers who make an event like this possible.

There are too many people to thank individually, and probably too many to count, but that's all right because the folks who work to keep Wenonah a vibrant community don't do it for recognition.

Let me just remind you of something you already know ... events like this just don't happen, and communities like Wenonah just don't happen. Our unique community is the culmination of a lot of hard work.

It's important to give some background of the award...

That's an important point in this year's Hometown Legend selection. This award was originated more than a decade ago by former NBA player and Wenonah resident Kevin Mullin, who wanted a mechanism to recognize, in the words of the award criteria, a person who "inspires legends, instills pride, and serves as a role model for the people of Wenonah."

Each year a current or former resident with a particular claim to fame has been selected for recognition by the Hometown Legends Committee.

Now we name the recipient but do not bring him up yet, to prevent awkwardness...

This year we are delighted to recognize Charles R. Forsman as our Hometown Legend winner.

[Point toward Chuck and hold for applause]

We know him as Chuck—or, for many years during the parade, Chuckles the Clown. Chuck holds nine patents—and, in recent years, has volunteered his talents to help solve environmental and infrastructure problems in the Wenonah area.

He lived in Wenonah for 42 years, has been married to his wife Lorrie for 59 years, and has worked in research, land development, affordable housing, and resource management.

He is an active community volunteer, and has played an important role in securing conservation land for Wenonah's "Ring of Green." He has worked on various projects on conservation lands.

Next, provide some time for you and the recipient to be photographed.

Please welcome to the mic ... Chuck Forsman.

[Hand over plaque and hold for applause]

And before I turn this over to Chuck, let me also note that after we decided on this award, an amazing event occurred that put Chuck's name in every paper in the region. For years he has been part of a group pushing for an improbable goal—acquiring an old abandoned golf course and getting it turned into a county park. Now—and I mean "now" as of last week—it's officially known as the Tall Pines Reservation.

Chuck, congratulations again, and let us know how all this came about ...

Source: Carl Hausman, delivered July 4, 2016, in Wenonah, NJ.

Afterword

I hope you've enjoyed this book and, more importantly, benefited from the content. Please check in from time to time at my Web site, CarlHausman .com, for more information related to effective communication, and feel free to subscribe to my Twitter feed, @carlhausman.

Appendix

A Presenter's Guide to Using and Understanding Statistics

Keep these 10 points in mind when wielding statistics.

1. DO NOT EQUATE A SPECIFIC-APPEARING NUMBER WITH ACCURACY

Just because something is worked out to two decimal places does not mean it conveys accurate or meaningful information. Remember, garbage in means garbage out. I might, for example, ask four people in Rochester, New York, how many hours per week they exercise. First of all, they are likely to lie to me, or at least stretch the truth, as most people will do when talking about how much they exercise or how little they eat. But suppose one person tells me "five hours," another says, "three hours," a third says, "maybe an hour and a half," and a fourth says, "nine." The mean average (see below for a definition of "mean") is 4.625.

When I inform you that "the average person in Rochester, New York, exercises 4.625 hours per week," it sounds like a well-researched number, even though it is simply "precision garbage." So when given a number as evidence, ask how that number was derived.

2. DETERMINE WHICH "AVERAGE" YOU ARE TALKING ABOUT

People interested in using averages to prove something will sometimes quote the average that is most favorable to them. "Average" can mean three different things:

- A mode, the most frequently occurring variable
- A median, the variable in the exact middle of a range of variables
- A mean, what you get when you add up everything and divide by the number of variables

Why are there different types of averages? There are good reasons for using different measures of how large collections of numbers tend to cluster around one value—or, as mathematicians would say, cluster around a "central tendency":

A **mode** gives you a good idea of the "average" grade for a college course. If, in a class of 33, there are three F's, five D's, fifteen C's, seven B's, and three A's, C is probably the fairest representative grade, because it occurs most often. Besides, you don't really have a way to mathematically add and divide letter grades.

A **median** is often used to convey the average of something when there are not many variables and there is a wide range in values. Real estate is a good example of proper use of a median. Simply adding up the cost of 11 homes that sold in a small town last month and dividing by 11 could produce a wildly inflated number if 10 of the homes sold for between $150,000 and $225,000 but number 11 was a mansion and sold for $3 million. Assume the houses sold for $155,000, $160,000, $170,000, $180,000, $180,000, $195,000, $195,000, $200,000, $220,000, $225,000, $230,000, and $3,000,000. Your arithmetical mean—what you get if you add up the price of the 11 houses and divide by 11—would be $446,000, which is not even close to a reasonable "average." But your median, the house that was right in the middle with five cheaper and five more expensive, would be $195,000.

A **mean** is most accurately representative when you are looking at a great deal of numbers and the numbers all mean the same thing. Average life span is a good example: a year is a year and dead is dead, and if you compute the mean for millions of people, you will get a reasonably meaningful number. (Remember, though, that there will be many variables in the mix, such as whether you add in infants who died in childbirth.)

There are also, of course, bad reasons for using different types of averages, the most common being persuasion or deception. It is not unusual for two sides in a labor dispute, for example, to come up with different "averages" for workers' salaries. The mode is often the lowest, the median the next highest, and the mean the highest. The choice of which one to cite can rest on what you are trying to prove.

On a related note, be careful of inferences from the word "average." Someone seeking election to a school board once inadvertently quoted Steven Wright by castigating the school administration because "half the reading scores in the district were below average." (Of course half were below average; in this case, average means the point where half are above and half are below.)

3. BE SKEPTICAL OF ANY FIGURE THAT MIXES APPLES AND ORANGES

What's wrong with this average?

The average person treated for a workplace-related injury by a chiropractor returned to work more quickly and spent less money on treatment than people who sought traditional medical care.

I have heard this claim made several times. It's probably true, but it's misleading because it mixes apples and oranges: people with minor injuries and people with major injuries. People with sore necks would be more likely to consult a chiropractor than would some poor wretch who had both legs torn off by a threshing machine. The fellow who lost both legs would certainly be seen by an emergency medical crew, a trauma surgeon, and a physical therapist. Recovery would take years—and would obviously cost a great deal of money.

4. NOTE THAT WHAT IS LEFT OUT OF A FIGURE IS AT LEAST AS IMPORTANT AS WHAT IS PUT IN

A few years ago, several major universities were caught inflating their average SAT score by leaving out people who did not score well on the test, such as international students whose native language was not English and thus didn't do very well on the verbal part of the test. Some colleges just dropped poor testers altogether, while others developed elaborate ruses, such as admitting them in August, not September, and thus keeping them off the books.

You can make a number say almost anything you want by leaving out components that work against you. Police departments, under pressure to lower crime rates, have been caught lowering the rates by simply not counting the actual crimes. Again, they sometimes developed ruses for doing this, such as reclassifying crime reports. What was once classified as a "theft" report became a "lost property" report. Or an auto theft report might be classified as "lost auto," which is the category usually used when someone can't remember where they parked their car at the mall.

5. CHECK COMPARISONS TO MAKE SURE THEY ARE, IN THE LITERAL SENSE OF THE WORK, COMPARABLE

Phone companies are notorious for running television commercials that use unbalanced comparisons. For example, one phone company may say that its rates for calling overseas are 40 percent lower than its competitor's, but it compares the rates on its international calling plan to those on its competitor's basic plan. Before regulators clamped down, phone-card companies were making numerical comparisons to the nonexistent, saying that their cards offered "more minutes" but not saying more minutes than what, or could "save you up to 70 percent"—leaving hanging the question, 70 percent of what?

6. IDENTIFY ANY VEILED VARIABLES USED TO CHANGE THE MEANING OR IMPACT OF THE NUMBER IN QUESTION

Let's continue with the phone company example, because their advertising makes use of cleverly veiled variables. One 10-10 calling service proclaimed that it charged 99 cents for calls "up to 20 minutes." Not a bad deal on its face, but remember that the "up to" means that if you get an answering machine and leave a brief message, you are basically paying more than a dollar a minute—more than it would cost you to call China with conventional phone service.

7. REMEMBER THAT POLLING DATA CAN BE SKEWED BY WHERE, WHEN, AND HOW THE QUESTIONS WERE ASKED, AND THAT CERTAIN THINGS CANNOT BE MEASURED VERY WELL

As a nation, we are addicted to polls, which have become one of the major ways we shape public policy. While polling data can be used to accurately measure and predict many quantities and qualities, polling does have limitations.

For example, you can almost literally reverse the answers to some questions by the way you phrase them. Ask, "Do you favor increasing benefits to disabled veterans, even though it will mean an increase in taxes?" and you will likely get a majority of "yes" respondents. Switch it around, asking, "Do you favor increasing taxes in order to increase benefits to disabled veterans?" and you are likely to get a majority of "no" answers.

You can skew the results of a poll depending on when and where you ask the questions. A poll conducted near the subway entrance at 6:00 AM is likely to snare a lot of respondents on their way to work at blue-collar jobs. People on the street at 1:00 PM near several swanky restaurants will likely give you a sample from a far different social spectrum, and those differences could be significant if you are measuring attitudes toward economic or labor issues.

Some beliefs and abstractions can't really be measured very well, such as generalized public opinion about an issue. Of course, some things can be measured with precision, such as the number of survey respondents who buy a specific model car. But we sometimes tend to think that attitudes can be measured with the accuracy of specific actions.

There is a deeper layer to this. Polls measure responses from people who may not know or may not care about the issue; they are confronted by a poll-taker and feel compelled to cough up an answer. Also, some people will tell you what they think you want to hear. The results may be statistically accurate but can hardly be interpreted as a measure of "public opinion." One of the best examples of this particular shortcoming was when a satire magazine named *Spy* polled U.S. congressional representatives about their attitudes toward the nation of Freedonia, pointing out, when the question was being asked, that the president felt that Freedonia was important to American interests. Many of the representatives replied that they, too, favored policy favorable to Freedonia.

The problem is that there's no country called Freedonia, except in the Marx Brothers movie *Duck Soup*, in which Groucho was appointed president.

8. FILTER OUT PROPORTION DISTORTION IN GRAPHS AND OTHER IMAGES

We are trained to think that seeing is believing, and that a graph or other visual compilation of data gives us an objective, unedited view of whatever it is we are trying to quantify. Don't believe that for a second—seeing is not believing. It's easy to tinker with a graph and make it say something not backed up by the data.

One of the best examples is the "Gee-Whiz graph," given its name by an author named Darrell Huff, who wrote the classic book *How to Lie with Statistics*. Making a Gee-Whiz graph is as simple as lopping off the bottom. For example, if I want to induce you to buy stock in my company, I must show you a graph of earnings that gives you the idea that profits are skyrocketing. Figure A.1 doesn't convey that impression.

But by amputating the bottom part of the graph and changing the relationship between the increments on the x and y axes, we get a genuine Gee-Whiz graph (Figure A.2) that makes it look like profits are shooting through the roof.

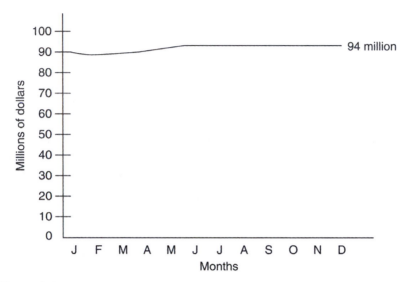

Figure A.1

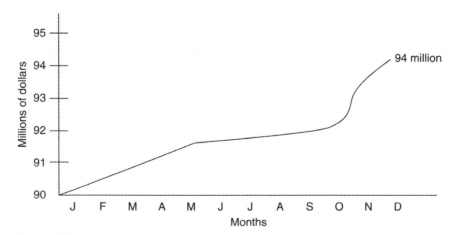

Figure A.2

9. WHEN SHOWN A GRAPH OR OTHER VISUAL REPRESENTATION, MAKE SURE IT COMMUNICATES SOMETHING OTHER THAN "THIS IS AN ATTEMPT TO MAKE YOU THINK THAT WHAT I'M SAYING IS SCIENTIFIC"

You'd be surprised how often nothing meaningful is communicated in a graphic. I remember a television ad for a pain reliever in which a graph labeled "pain relief" shot skyward. But there was no mention of what was actually being measured. Pain-ograms?

10. NO MATTER HOW TEMPTING, DO NOT AUTOMATICALLY ASSUME A CAUSE-AND-EFFECT RELATIONSHIP BETWEEN EVENTS THAT FOLLOW ONE ANOTHER, AND DO NOT AUTOMATICALLY ASSUME THAT THEY ARE STATISTICALLY LINKED

Just because Event A happened and Event B followed, you can't always assume that Event A caused Event B. After all, a rooster crowed this morning, and then the sun came up; that doesn't mean the rooster caused the sunrise. If Event A and Event B seem to be linked statistically, it still does not mean there is necessarily a cause-and-effect relationship, because other variables may be the part of the linkage. For example, it is an indisputable fact that married men, on average, live longer than unmarried men. But can you assume, as more than one magazine article writer has, that "Loneliness Kills"? Perhaps it does, but there are many other factors that may account for why single men die younger than married men:

- Men born with chronic illnesses may never marry or may die at a young age
- Many young men are killed in accidents before they reach marriage age
- In wartime, single men are often drafted instead of married men and obviously stand a greater risk of dying in combat

In summary, always hunt for alternate reasons why two events may be linked, and question any assumption of cause and effect.[1]

Notes

CHAPTER 1

1. James C. Humes, *Eisenhower and Churchill: The Partnership That Saved the World* (New York: Three Rivers Press, 2001).

2. Melissa Carter, "Using Needs Assessment to Choose the Target Audience," https://lsuagcenterode.wordpress.com/2011/09/07/using-needs-assessment-to-choose-the-target-audience (accessed May 1, 2016).

3. Edward R. Murrow, "A Report on Sen. Joseph McCarthy," http://www.lib.berkeley.edu/MRC/murrowmccarthy.html (accessed July 12, 2016).

4. "Life After Death by PowerPoint," https://www.youtube.com/watch?v=MjcO2ExtHso (accessed July 12, 2016).

CHAPTER 2

1. "Screenwriting: Lecture by Stephen J. Cannell, http://www.writerswrite.com/screenwriting/cannell/lecture4 (accessed July 12, 2016).

2. Joshua Gowin, PhD, "Why Sharing Stories Brings People Together," *Psychology Today*, https://www.psychologytoday.com/blog/you-illuminated/201106/why-sharing-stories-brings-people-together?collection=67103 (accessed June 6, 2011).

3. Allison Goldberg and Jen Jamula, "Five Ways to Give a Presentation That Nobody Will Ever Forget," *Inc.*, http://www.inc.com/allison-goldberg-jen-jamula/5-ways-to-give-a-presentation-that-no-one-will-ever-forget.html (accessed July 12, 2016).

4. "Ethos, Pathos, Logos: The Three Rhetorical Appeals," http://georgehwilliams.pbworks.com/w/page/14266873/Ethos-Pathos-Logos-The-3-Rhetorical-Appeals (accessed July 12, 2016).

5. Daniel Tenner, "How to Use the Power of Silence to Be Heard," Lifehacker, http://lifehacker.com/5831374/how-to-use-the-power-of-silence-to-be-heard (accessed July 12, 2016).

6. Alex Shepard, "Minutes," *New Republic,* https://newrepublic.com/minutes/126677/it-aint-dont-know-gets-trouble-must-big-short-opens-fake-mark-twain-quote (accessed July 12, 2016).

7. Don Shirley, "Why Don't Plays Start on Time?" *Los Angeles Times,* http://articles.latimes.com/2003/aug/10/entertainment/ca-shirley10 (accessed July 12, 2016).

CHAPTER 3

1. Olivia Mitchell, "Eight Presentation Tips to Make Your Eye Contact More Powerful,"   http://www.speakingaboutpresenting.com/delivery/tips-eye-contact (accessed July 12, 2016).

2. Reid Buckley, *Strictly Speaking* (McGraw-Hill, 1999), p. 6.

3. "Using Statistics in Your Speech," http://www.cfug-md.org/speakertips/783.html (accessed July 12, 2106).

4. Brian Tracy, "Nine Tips to End Your Speech with a Bang," http://www.briantracy.com/blog/public-speaking/how-to-end-a-speech-the-right-way (accessed July 12, 2016).

CHAPTER 4

1. Olivia Mitchell, "How to Handle a Heckler," http://www.speakingabout presenting.com/audience/handle-a-heckler (accessed July 12, 2016).

CHAPTER 5

1. "Teach Every Child About Food," https://www.ted.com/talks/jamie_oliver (accessed July 12, 2016).

2. Stanford News, https://news.stanford.edu/2005/06/14/jobs-061505 (accessed July 14, 2016).

3. Brian Tracy, "Fifteen Ways to Start a Speech," http://www.briantracy.com/blog/public-speaking/how-to-start-a-speech (accessed July 15, 2016).

CHAPTER 6

1. "Tips for Creating and Delivering an Effective Presentation," https://support.office.com/en-us/article/Tips-for-creating-and-delivering-an-effective-presentation-f43156b0-20d2-4c51-8345-0c337cefb88b (accessed July 15, 2016).

2. Todd Bishop, "Bill Gates' Mosquito Stunt," *Puget Sound Business Journal,* http://www.bizjournals.com/seattle/blog/techflash/2009/02/Bill_Gates_mosquito_stunt_What_really_happened39115792.html (accessed July 15, 2016).

CHAPTER 7

1. Sue Schellenbarger, "Is This How You Really Talk?" *Wall Street Journal,* http://www.wsj.com/articles/SB10001424127887323735604578440851083674898 (accessed July 15, 2016).

2. "Want a Promotion? Don't Speak Like an Aussie," *Daily Mail,* http://www.dailymail.co.uk/sciencetech/article-2538554/Want-promotion-Dont-speak-like-AUSSIE-Rising-pitch-end-sentences-make-sound-insecure.html (accessed July 15, 2016).

CHAPTER 8

1. Jeffrey Brewer, "Snakes Top List of Americans' Fears," http://www.gallup.com/poll/1891/snakes-top-list-americans-fears.aspx (accessed July 15, 2016).

CHAPTER 9

1. Suzette Martinez Standring, "Being Funny, Dave Barry Style," http://www.columnists.com/2008/04/being-funny-dave-barry-style (accessed July 15, 2016).

2. John Brandon, "Sixteen Funny Quotes to Start Your Next Business Presentation," http://www.inc.com/john-brandon/16-funny-quotes-to-start-your-next-business-presentation.html (accessed July 15, 2016).

3. Suzette Martinez Standring, "Being Funny, Dave Barry Style," http://www.columnists.com/2008/04/being-funny-dave-barry-style (accessed July 15, 2016).

4. Carl Hausman, *Write Like a Pro* (Santa Barbara: Praeger, 2016), pp. 53–54.

5. Lisa B. Marshall, "How to Make People Laugh During a Presentation," http://www.quickanddirtytips.com/business-career/public-speaking/how-to-make-people-laugh-during-presentations (accessed July 15, 2016).

CHAPTER 10

1. Nancy Vogt, "Podcasting Fact Sheet," http://www.journalism.org/2015/04/29/podcasting-fact-sheet-2015 (accessed July 15, 2016).

2. Jesse Noyes, "Should Your Company Start a Podcast?" *Harvard Business Review,* https://hbr.org/2014/12/should-your-company-start-a-podcast (accessed July 15, 2016).

3. "Suze Orman Biography," http://www.biography.com/people/suze-orman-524060#aspiring-restauranteur (accessed July 15, 2016).

CHAPTER 11

1. "Give Me Liberty or Give Me Death," https://www.history.org/almanack/life/politics/giveme.cfm (accessed July 15, 2016).

CHAPTER 12

1. Newton N. Minow, "Television and the Public Interest," http://www
.americanrhetoric.com/speeches/newtonminow.htm (accessed July 15, 2016).

2. "Give Me Liberty or Give Me Death," https://en.m.wikisource.org/wiki/Give
_me_liberty_or_give_me_death (accessed July 15, 2016).

APPENDIX

1. Carl Hausman, "How to Think About Information," personally published
educational material reprinted with the permission of the author. Me.

Further Reading

Here are some resources you will find helpful. Books are republished frequently in many formats, so I will just list the author and title. For Web sites, I will just list the topmost relevant page, because the deeper links may go dead.

BOOKS

Reid Buckley, *Strictly Speaking*
Jeremy Donovan, *How to Deliver a TED Talk: Secrets of the World's Most Inspiring Presentations*
John Dumas, *Podcast Launch: A Complete Guide to Launching Your Podcast with 15 Video Tutorials*
Milo O. Frank, *How to Get Your Point Across in 30 Seconds or Less*
Carl Hausman, *Write Like a Pro*
James C. Humes, *Speak Like Churchill, Stand Like Lincoln: 21 Powerful Secrets of History's Greatest Speakers*

WEB SITES

memory.loc.gov/ammem/nfhtml/nfhome.html
www.americanrhetoric.com
www.4uth.gov.ua/usa/english/facts/speeches.htm
www.TED.com

Index

About the Author

CARL HAUSMAN, PhD, is professor of journalism at Rowan University in Glassboro, New Jersey, and author of 20 books, including *Write Like a Pro* (Praeger, 2016). He has appeared in many venues, including *The O'Reilly Factor*, *Anderson Cooper's World News Now*, CBS Radio's *Capitol Voices*, and other network and local television and radio programs. Hausman has testified before Congress, delivered thousands of lectures and presentations, narrated eight audiobooks, and taught a variety of writing, speaking, and broadcast announcing courses. He is national chair of the broadcast journalism judging panel for the National Headliner Awards, one of the nation's oldest and largest awards programs recognizing journalism excellence. His Web site is www.carlhausman.com, and his Twitter feed is @carlhausman.